ARTICLES

ON EMPLOYMENT LAW,

CREDIT LAW,

AND

GENERAL BUSINESS LAW

WRITTEN

BY

JAMES H. HOPKINS JD SPHR

©James H. Hopkins 2016

Over a career in the Legal Profession and Human Resources that spanned five decades I have written numerous ARTICLES on various topics. I have included them here in this volume.

This volume and all else in my career is dedicated to my dear wife Evie, who supported me throughout.

ABOUT THE AUTHER

James H. (Jim) Hopkins received a Bachelors of General Studies with an emphasis in Economics from the University of Nebraska at Omaha, did Graduate Studies in Economics at the University of Nebraska at Omaha and received a Juris Doctorate from the University of Puget Sound in Tacoma Washington.

Mr. Hopkins has forty plus years of experience in the Construction Industry and in the field of Employer/Employee Relations. The employee/employer relations experience is as a Human Resource Professional and as a practicing Attorney.

Mr. Hopkins also serves as an arbitrator and a mediator for business, employment and labor disputes.

Mr. Hopkins Lectures on employment law and other business/construction related topics including ethics at Seattle Pacific University, Bellevue College and Edmonds Community College, all in the greater Seattle area. He has written numerous articles and publications in the area of human resources and construction and has published three books, "Human Resource-Labor Relations A Primer", "Construction Liens for the Pacific Northwest Alaska Idaho Oregon Washington Federal Public Works A Primer" and "Employment Law for Washington State A Primer".

TABLE OF CONTENTS

FIVE STEPS CREDIT MANAGERS CAN TAKE TO INCREASE RECOVERY OF RECEIVABLES..............................8

CREATING A COMPETITIVE SAFETY NET THROUGH THE USE OF NO-COMPETE AGREEMENTS WITH EMPLOYEES.........13

THE USE OF ALTERNATIVE DISPUTE RESOLUTION (ADR) BY THE CREDIT PROFESSIONAL...........19

ELECTRONIC MAIL AND THE CREDIT EXECUTIVE......................................25

THE EMPLOYER/EMPLOYEE RELATIONSHIP IN THE NEW MILLENIUM: REPLACING WASHINGTON STATE'S AILING EMPLOYMENT AT WILL DOCTRINE.....................................29

ETHICAL CONCERNS FOR THE CREDIT MANAGER......................................47

WHEN IT COMES TO CONSTRUCTION LIENS, STRICT COMPLIANCE IS REQUIRED......................................51

MECHANIC'S and MATERIALMAN'S LIENS in WASHINGTON...............................63

USING THE MILLER ACT TO COLLECT ON
FEDERAL PROJECTS............................75

REVISITING THE MILLER ACT:
COLLECTIONS ON FEDERAL PROJECTS.80

NEGOTIATIONS AND THE CREDIT
PROFESSIONAL..................................86

THE NATIONAL LABOR RELATIONS ACT
AND NON-UNION EMPLOYERS.............92

TIMELY PAYMENT ON CONSTRUCTION
PROJECTS...97

SUCCESSFULLY PROSECUTING
CONSTRUCTION CLAIMS
BEFORE DISPUTES ARISE....................102

USING THE EICHLEAY FORMULA TO
CALCULATE HOME OFFICE OVERHEAD
ON CONSTRUCTION DELAY CLAIMS....106

DAMAGES WHICH FLOW FROM THE
BREACH OF A CONSTRUCTION
CONTRACT..111

CREDIT TODAY DOCTOR CREDIT
COLUMN..116

THE "ECONOMIC LOSS DOCTRINE" IN
WASHINGTON……………………………..118

EMPLOYEE MISCONDUCT AND SAFETY
PROGRAMS……………………………...122

THE EMPLOYER/EMPLOYEE
RELATIONSHIP BEGINS BEFORE THE
BEGINNING……………………….……..126

THE FAIR LABOR STANDARDS ACT
(FLSA) A BOOK REVIEW…………………132

INDIVIDUAL LIABILTY FOR CORPORATE
ACTS BY BOARD OF DIRECTORS POST
ENRON/WORLDCOM……………………..137

MECHANIC'S AND MATERIALMAN'S
LIENS -- STRICT COMPLIANCE WITH
STATUTE REQUIRED……………………..143

LIMITATIONS OF LIABILITY CLAUSES:
IGNORANCE IS NOT BLISS………………146

MANAGING EMPLOYEE ABSENTISM
IN WASHINGTON…………………………151

MEDICAL PROFESSION UNIONIZED
RULES IN A NONUNION
ENVIRONMENT……………………………158

MILITARY VETERAN'S REEMPLOYMENT RIGHTS…………………………………...162

NEGOTIATIONS AND THE HUMAN RESOURCE PROFESSIONAL……………..166

THE PENALTIES EMPLOYERS FACE FOR VIOLATING THE NATIONAL LABOR RELATIONS ACT (NLRA)…………………172

CONSTRUCTION SITE SAFETY WHO IS RESPONSIBLE?.............................176

THE FAIR CREDIT REPORTING ACT (FCRA) AND
THE INVESTIGATION OF EMPLOYEE MISCONDUCT……………………...……181

ARTICLE NINE OF THE UNIFORM COMMERCIAL CODE MEETS CYBERSPACE………………………….183

A PRIMER ON PURCHASE MONEY SECURITY INTERESTS (PMSI) UNDER THE UNIFORM COMMERCIAL CODE…………………………………….186

YOU TAKE THE GAVEL; BATTLE OF THE FORMS……………………….....………190

YOU TAKE THE GAVEL; WHEN IS A PREFERENCE A PREFERENCE IN BANKRUPTCY PROCEEDINGS...............194

YOU TAKE THE GAVEL……………………..196

YOU TAKE THE GAVEL……………………..198

YOU TAKE THE GAVEL;
WHEN "PAYMENT IN FULL" MEANS JUST THAT………………………………………....…200

YOU TAKE THE GAVEL; WHEN IS A CONTRACT A CONTRACT……………..…..204

YOU TAKE THE GAVEL……………………..207

FIVE STEPS CREDIT MANAGERS CAN TAKE TO INCREASE RECOVERY OF RECEIVABLES

BY: James H. Hopkins JD SPHR

There are a variety of reasons Credit Managers encounter difficulties in collecting 100% of Accounts Receivable, many of which are beyond the Credit Department's control. There are, however, a number of steps a Credit Manager can take to realize a larger recovery percentage. This article explores five of these steps.

1. Have An Executed Credit Application On File

Many times, especially with new customers, products are shipped and receivables are on the books before the paper work is complete. Frequently, missing paper work is an executed credit application. If the credit application is executed after the goods are shipped, there is a distinct probability that its terms and conditions will not be enforceable on the goods shipped prior to its execution. Other situations occur where the credit application is not reviewed until there is a dispute; only to discover the debtor's signature is missing. An unsigned agreement can restrict the Credit Manager from recovering interest and/or carrying charges. In the event the unsigned credit application contained an attorneys' fees clause, the legal fees to pursue the debtor would likely be unrecoverable also. Obviously, not having a signed credit application prior to doing business may cut into the firm's profit should disputes arise.

>   2.   Ensure Personal Guarantees Are Signed In An Individual Not Corporate Capacity

A lot of Credit Managers insist that a small or closely-held corporation execute a personal guarantee before credit is extended. This is highly recommended and often will increase the likelihood of recovery. However, the personal guarantee may be of little worth if the guarantor signs the document in their corporate capacity, i.e. Jane Doe, President. By signing in this manner, Jane Doe has executed the personal guarantee as a corporate officer, not as an individual, and therefore would probably not be held individually liable for any outstanding debt.

>   3.   Incorporate An Attorneys' Fees Clause Into The Terms And Conditions of The Credit Application

Although an attorneys' fees clause does not affect the ability to collect the principal amount of a receivable, it does ensure that the Credit Manager will be entitled to recover attorneys' fees as part of the collection process. Generally, there are only two ways in which a party can recover attorneys' fees during the collection process: (1) when a statute authorizes it; or (2) when the parties agree in writing.

Statutory authority is seldom found in the collection arena. The Credit Manager must instead rely upon the contract with the customer. The contract document will generally be a credit application, which should contain a provision for the award of attorney's fees to the prevailing party.

A sample attorneys' fees clause is:
In the event there is any dispute hereunder, seller shall be entitled to recover attorney's fees plus costs, including attorney's fees and costs for appeal and collection of any judgment obtained.

4. Hold A Debtor To Their Credit Terms

Credit Managers may find themselves working with a debtor who keeps in constant contact and gives assurances that in just a few days -- a week at the most -- the bill will be paid. Given the debtor's apparent good faith in resolving the outstanding debt, the Credit Manager may let the debt slide beyond the ordinary credit terms established with the debtor and outside the ordinary credit terms of the creditor's industry before being paid. It may be said, and rightfully so, "what difference does that make, I got paid." However, should the debtor file for bankruptcy protection, problems may arise if the debtor made a payment within the 90-day period prior to the bankruptcy filing, and payment is not in the ordinary course of business between the parties or is outside of industry standards. The payment that the Credit Manager was so glad to receive may have to be returned. Credit Managers must do all that is possible to hold a debtor to their credit terms or at the very least, keep the receivable from getting any larger.

5. Ensure That Purchase Orders Are Complete

Many purchase orders are received from debtors via the fax machine. The individual faxing the purchase order and the recipient at the creditor's office are only concerned about two things -- price and quantity. Generally, the terms and conditions of the sale (i.e., late fees, payment terms, and attorney fees clauses) are found on the back side of the purchase order and may never get faxed. Once again, this leaves the Credit Manager with the inability to enforce those terms against the debtor. Every Credit Manager must insure that the dreaded paper work is complete before the product is shipped.

Conclusion

These suggestions are by no means exhaustive. Viewed on paper, they appear quite simple; however, the difficulty arises in the consistent implementation of these steps. A Credit Manager should strive to incorporate these steps into their day-to-day credit practices.

CREATING A COMPETITIVE SAFETY NET THROUGH THE USE OF NO-COMPETE AGREEMENTS WITH EMPLOYEES

By: James H. Hopkins, J.D., S.P.H.R.*

Introduction

A recent Wall Street Journal article addressed the increased instances of employers attempting to enforce no-compete agreements against former employees.

There may be many reasons for this, but I believe the most prevalent is that "start-up businesses" of the '90's are able to compete effectively with more established companies within the same industry by having the "right" personnel, i.e., "brain capital". This will not diminish as we move into the new millennium.

Employers' Concerns

- With the advent of technology, employees are obtaining greater access to and knowledge of an employer's customer lists and processes, etc. than ever in the past.

- Large numbers of start-up companies are springing to life, particularly in the high-tech sector, and the loss of a single key employee to a competitor can have a devastating effect on a company.

• Employees are not staying with a single employer throughout their career.
The concept of cradle to grave employment is a part of a bygone era.

These are but a few of the reasons employers have become more protective of the experience and training they provide to employees. One of the ways of protecting the information and training to employees requires employees to execute one or more agreements as a condition of employment.

Agreements

There are three general types of agreements which an employer may require an employee to sign at the beginning of the employer/employee relationship in order to minimize the concerns expressed above. Such agreements are: (1) No-compete Agreement; (2) Confidentiality Agreement; and (3) Assignment of Invention Agreement.

No-compete Agreements

Historically, no-compete agreements have been for top-level employees, but the trend is to have individuals throughout the company hierarchy sign such documents. The intent of the no-compete agreement is to eliminate potential of a departing employee from competing or working for a competitor of the ex-employer. This is accomplished by restricting him or her from working in a particular industry and/or in a designated area in the same or similar capacity for a specified period of time.

In Washington, a no-compete agreement will be enforced when the restraint of an employee's ability to work is necessary to protect the business goodwill of a previous employer. A court will balance the interest of the company against the interest of the individual and look to who bears the greater hardship if the agreement is not enforced. When the greatest hardship falls on the former employer, the agreement will be enforced. The courts will also look at whether enforcement of the no-compete agreement will deprive an individual of his or her ability to produce a livelihood.

In addition, it is necessary that the damage to the general public's loss of services of an individual must be less than the problems created by the former employee competing with his/her previous employer. In this situation, an individual trained in a field where many people possess the same skill is more apt to have a no-compete agreement enforced against him or her than when someone who possesses one-of-a-kind skill.

Courts in Washington have enforced no-compete agreements for periods up to and including three years in duration. Enforcement is also generally limited to a specific geographic area.

The enforcement of no-compete agreements is clearly fact specific.

Confidential Agreements

Confidentiality agreements generally go hand-in-hand with no-compete agreements. A confidentiality agreement between an employer and an employee establishes up-front that an employer intends to protect its internal business/trade secrets.

Trade secrets are defined and protected by statute in Washington. It is improper, whether there is a confidentiality agreement or not, to disclose a trade secret. A trade secret is defined as something that has novelty, and is not readily available to the public. A properly executed confidentiality agreement may go beyond this interpretation, as long as the employer doesn't overreach.

Assignment of Invention.

The third area that may be covered in an agreement between employers and employees is an assignment of his or her rights to any inventions.

Assignment of the rights to an invention by an employee to an employer is governed by statute in the State of Washington. An employer cannot insist an employee assign any right to an invention; when the invention was developed by the employee on the employee's own time; with his or her own efforts and where no employer facilities were utilized, and the invention doesn't apply to the employer's business. In addition, any agreement regarding the assignment of inventions to an employer must provide clear notice of the assignment to the employee.

In the event any portion of an agreement assigning any rights to an invention is found to violate public policy, not only will the offending section be unenforceable, but the entire agreement will be voided unless the agreement contains a severability clause.

A severability clause basically states that if any section of the contract is found to be void for any reason, only the offending section is void. The balance of the agreement would be enforceable.

Conclusion

Any employer wishing to have an agreement covering any or all of these topics should first evaluate its necessity. If the decision is then made to proceed with such an agreement, the agreement should be written in such a manner to protect the parties' interests and comply with all the requisite laws.

This area of the employer/employee relationship needs to be handled with the same professionalism and sensitivity as any other area within that relationship.

* Mr. Hopkins represents business clients in all areas of matters relating to business and commercial transactions, as well as situations relating to the employer/employee relationship. Mr. Hopkins has 20 years' experience assisting business in these areas.

THE USE OF ALTERNATIVE DISPUTE RESOLUTION (ADR) BY THE CREDIT PROFESSIONAL

By: James H. Hopkins JD SPHR

The credit professional's role is to collect monies due their company. When a customer does not pay in a timely manner or does not pay at all, the credit professional may pursue alternatives to litigation to resolve such disputes. The major reason for seeking alternatives to litigation is cost, followed closely by time. Dispute resolution may also be sought when an ongoing customer has an account in dispute and the effects of litigating would cause greater harm to the business relationship.

Alternative dispute resolution (ADR) generally consists of three methods: 1) negotiation; 2) mediation; and 3) arbitration. The focus here will be on mediation and arbitration as methods for resolving disputes.

Disputes arise when the creditor and debtor's views differ as to whether money is owed. Maintaining an objective evaluation of one's position in such a situation can be very difficult and may require a neutral third party to assist in the process. This neutral third party may either be a mediator or an arbitrator.

The use of mediation as a form of dispute resolution must be part of the original contract between the parties. The courts will not force a party to use mediation unless they have contractually agreed to such a program; however, some court rules require mediation before trial.

Just as in mediation, the parties seeking resolution through arbitration must reach agreement to arbitrate at the beginning of the relationship rather than attempting to reach such an agreement after a dispute arises. The courts will enforce an arbitration agreement. This means if the parties agree to an arbitration clause in their contract, the courts will say arbitration must be used to resolve their disputes. In the same way, a court will not overturn an arbitrator's award, unless there is some egregious reason to do so. It is clear that the best time, if not the only time, to reach an agreement, even on how to resolve disputes, is at the beginning of the relationship, not when a dispute arises.

Mediation

In mediation, a neutral third party assists in the negotiations to resolve a dispute. In order to be successful, mediation must have certain things happen: 1) the parties must have those individuals present at the mediation who have authority to settle the dispute; and 2) the individuals at the mediation must be objective regarding settlement, bring a broad perspective, and be open to finding creative solutions to the dispute. Without this, the possibility of resolution is doomed before it begins.

The mediation process consists of preparation, an initial meeting, recess, and follow-up meetings. Part of the preparation phase will be the selecting a mediator. This is one of the most critical components of the mediation process, as the mediator will be acting as an impartial, objective participant in the negotiations. If the mediator is not swayed by a party's arguments, the party may not be successful in convincing an arbitrator, a judge or jury. The proper choice of a mediator will be someone who possesses both an understanding of the issues, and the confidence of the parties involved.

Mediators can be obtained from various sources. The local bar association will have available names of prospective mediators, as well as various legal and/or industry associations, or the parties may just pick a person known to the parties.

Depending upon the mediator's preference, the initial meeting may be held with all the parties and the mediator present, or with the parties separately. If separated, the mediator will shuttle between the parties until an agreement is reached or an impasse develops. Mediation will only be successful if there is a dollar amount in common in the parties' settlement ranges.

Arbitration

Arbitration differs from mediation in that the arbitrator, a neutral third party, will issue a binding decision, whereas the mediator can only assist the parties into reaching an agreed-upon resolution.

The arbitrator can be selected in the same manner as a mediator. There may be a single arbitrator of multiple arbitrators, depending upon what the parties have agreed to in the arbitration agreement.

The arbitration process is quite different from the mediation process in that it is an adversarial hearing where witnesses will be examined and cross-examined in much the same way a court trial would be conducted. The Procedural Rules for the arbitration hearing is in the hands of the arbitrator. Generally, the hearing will follow the format of a less formal trial, with each side giving an opening statement, then the party demanding arbitration will put on their case. This will usually include witness testimony and the introduction of documents. The defending party will have the opportunity to cross-examine any witness. Then the defending party will have its opportunity to present its case. The arbitrator will then render an opinion.

Online ADR

Bringing alternative dispute resolution into the 21st century is online ADR, which utilizes the internet as a means to more efficiently engage parties in non-litigious dispute resolution. Online ADR resolves disputes by harnessing computer-networking technology to bring parties together in a dialogue that is usually hosted by a third party service provider. Similar to traditional ADR, Online ADR can come in the form of binding or non-binding decisions. Non-binding decisions just like traditional mediation allows the parties to seek further redress if a party feels that a just decision cannot been reached.

Typically, the Online ADR process begins when a claimant registers with an Online ADR Provider. The ADR Provider then uses the information provided by the claimant to contact the defendant party and invite them to participate in Online ADR. If the defendant accepts the invitation, they will file an online response to the claimant's complaint. From this point, the various ADR Providers take on different approaches. Some have developed proprietary software that allows parties to engage in negotiation of monetary sums without the participation of a third party.

Other service providers have taken a more hands-on approach that provides for other traditional mediation services across email and interactive web sites. Still others employ variations of these two methods. Another area of difference is the level of enforceability of a settlement. While most online settlements are not legally binding and enforceable, some ADR providers require or encourage parties to enter into a binding settlement contract. Of course, such a settlement is only enforceable to the extent allowed by various state contract laws.

ELECTRONIC MAIL AND THE CREDIT EXECUTIVE

By: James H. Hopkins JD SPHR

Advances in technology are creating new opportunities as well as new challenges for businesses. Today what we take for granted to help get our jobs done quickly and efficiently was no more than fantasy less than a decade ago. Just five years ago, most business professionals had never even heard of the Internet, yet now 90% of full-time, four-year college students in the U.S. report using the Internet.

Even though the internet wasn't commercially available until the early 1990s, its use by both individuals and businesses has exploded. One of the biggest impacts of internet use to businesses has been electronic mail (e-mail). In 1998, the U.S. Postal Service delivered 107 billion pieces of First Class Mail. During the same year, 3.4 trillion e-mail messages were delivered electronically. This equates to 9.4 billion messages exchanged every day of the year in the U.S. alone -- on average, individuals in the U.S. sent or received 26.4 e-mail messages every day in 1998. The electronic age of communication is here.

While the appearance of e-mail on the business scene means that work can be completed faster than ever before, there is a tendency to be informal and less guarded in electronic mail than other written forms of mail. This casual attitude in electronic correspondence should be of concern for the credit manager.

E-mail is forever

It is assumed that once an e-mail is deleted from the computer, it has been erased from existence – similar to shredding a paper document. Nothing is further from reality. Even if both sender and recipient delete a message, it may remain on a number of computers through which the e-mail passed on its way to delivery. These e-mails can be restored and used during litigation. Consider that approximately 85% of the Iran-contra hearing evidence was the result of restored e-mail. Microsoft has found itself damaged with the introduction of internal messages as evidence in its antitrust case. Obviously, these examples represent high-profile cases with large litigation budgets which include monies to retrieve electronic information. However, the discovery of electronic records, including computer hard drives, is commonplace in the everyday world of litigation. Companies now are routinely required to produce computerized information during litigation just as they are required to produce hard copies of memos and documentation.

Without an adequate policy concerning the use and storage of electronic medium, a company may find the very technology which helped it grow and succeed will become its enemy should damaging electronic documents be discovered during the course of litigation.

Clearly, starting to shred evidence after the commencement of a dispute is destruction of evidence. But an acceptable business practice is to regularly destroy paper and/or electronic documents.

Establish an E-Policy

To guard against potential e-problems, companies should develop an overall policy for dealing with electronic mail. Such a policy should identify: (1) computer ownership; (2) prohibited uses; (3) wastes of company resources; (4) lack of expectation of privacy; (5) address employers right to monitor; and (6) care in drafting e-mail. The policy should clearly establish that employees are to use the same quality of writing e-mail as in any other written communication.

In addition to a formal e-mail policy, the company should develop a computerized information retention policy, which can be incorporated into an overall records retention policy. The retention policy for computerized information should contain a specified time for retaining documents. Once the timeframe has expired, the electronic information should be automatically deleted. Employees should also be directed to regularly discard stored computerized communications. Furthermore, employees ought to be instructed to suspend the automatic deletion process during litigation or investigation of suspected litigation.

A new company purports to have developed a way for e-mail to evaporate or self-destruct on all computers through which it passes anywhere from seconds to decades after being transmitted depending on the sender's preferences. This technology is not yet on the market. Until such technology is standard, it is imperative that credit professionals take a proactive approach to their electronic transmissions and recordkeeping before being forced into action by a costly court battle.

THE EMPLOYER/EMPLOYEE RELATIONSHIP IN THE NEW MILLENIUM: REPLACING WASHINGTON STATE'S AILING EMPLOYMENT AT WILL DOCTRINE

By: James H. Hopkins, JD SPHR

In 1928, the Washington State Supreme Court established the Employment at Will Doctrine in an effort to set forth a standard by which employers and employees could define the employment relationship.[1] In its simplest form, the doctrine provides that when no definite time period was contracted for, the employer or employee could terminate the employment relationship at any time for any reason or for no reason.[2]

Since it was first pronounced, the doctrine has undergone a radical metamorphosis. Through the gradual removal of its underpinnings by the Legislature, Congress, and the Courts, the doctrine today is no longer recognizable as set forth in 1928.

More than twenty years ago, the Washington State Supreme Court recognized the mutable nature of the Employment at Will Doctrine when it stated: "While the future of this doctrine is a compelling issue, it is one that must be left for another day and different facts."[3]

Furthermore, progressive business leaders are not utilizing the doctrine. Instead, they are developing "... provisions for employment security, ... and practices reflecting the organization's concern for the general well-being of the employee and his/her family."[4]

Replacing the stripped-down doctrine with a new standard that incorporates the changes made by the Legislature and the Courts, as well as private employers seems timely.

[1]Davidson v. Machall-Paine Veneer Co., 149 Wn. 685 (1928) at 688.

[2]Ibid.

[3]Robert V. Atlantic Richfield Company, 88 Wn.2nd 887 (1977), at 898.

[4]Paul R. Lawrence, Davis Dyer, Renewing American Industry, 1983 at 11.

A HISTORICAL PERSPECTIVE OF THE EMPLOYMENT AT WILL DOCTRINE

The Employment at Will concept, as first enunciated in Washington State, stated: "The law of the cases seems to be well settled, that a contract such as this constitutes an employment for an indefinite period and that such a contract may be abandoned by either party at will without incurring any liability therefore."[5]

In deciding that the law was "well settled," the court relied upon H.G. Wood's commentary that: "A mere promise to work for another, no time or terms being fixed, is not a contract for service, for a breach of which an action will lie."[6]

Mr. Wood relied upon British law when making his statement; specifically, "That one must be bound to employ, and the other to serve, for a certain definite time, . . . and there is no contract of hiring and service obligatory beyond the will of either party."[7]

The statements expressed by Mr. Wood and the cases he relied upon conflict with other English cases of that time period which held that any hiring that was not for a definite period of time was for one year. Mr. Blackstone stated: "If the hiring be general, without any particular time limited, the law construes it to be a hiring for a year; ..."[8] These conflicting statements raise the question of how "well settled"[9] the law was in 1928 when the Washington State Supreme Court established the Employment at Will Doctrine.

The Employment at Will theory was addressed in other commentaries: "It is a part of every man's civil rights that he be left at liberty to refuse business relations with any person whom so ever, whether the refusal rests upon reason or is a result of whim, capriciousness prejudice or malice."[10]

[5] Davidson v. Machall-Paine Veneer Co., supra. at 688 emphasis added.

[6] H.G. Wood, "A Treatise on the Law of Master and Servant" (1877) at 157-158.

[7] Williamson v. Taylor, 5 Q.B. 175, cited in Mr. Wood's commentary at 157.

[8] "Blackstone's Commentaries on the Laws of England", edited by T.M. Cooley, (1879), Book 1 page 424.

[9] For one Courts questioning of Woods formulation see Toussand v. Blue Cross & Blue Shield of Mich. 408 Mich. 579 (1980)

[10] T.M. Cooley, "A treatise of the law of torts", (1880), page 278.

The sentiment expressed by Mr. Cooley above fit the judicial philosophy of "laissez-faire constitutionalism" of that time, and was characterized by the U.S. Supreme Court's attitude between the 1860's and the 1930's.[11] It was during this period that the U.S. Supreme Court struck down a statute, which made it unlawful to discriminate against employees based on union membership. The Court held ". . . so the right of employee to quit the service of the employer for whatever reason is the same as the right of the employer, for whatever reason, to dispense with the services of such employee."[12] The Court continued:

> "In all such particulars (referring to either the employer or employee terminating the employment relationship) the employer and the employee have equality of right, and any legislation that disturbs that equality is an arbitrary interference with the liberty of contract which no Government can legally justify in a free land."[13]

Justice Holmes dissented, stating: "The section simply prohibits the more powerful party to extract certain undertakings, or to threaten dismissal or unjustly discriminate on certain grounds on those already employed."[14] He went on to state "Where there is, or generally is believed to be, an important ground of public policy for restraint, the constitution does not forbid it".[15]

EXCEPTIONS TO THE EMPLOYMENT AT WILL DOCTRINE

Since the inception of the Employment at Will Doctrine, an employer could not terminate an employee when an employment contract for a specified period of time existed, without complying with the terms of the contract.[16] Thus, there has always been an "express contract" exception to the doctrine. Another exception to the Employment at Will Doctrine is a contract implied from the attendant circumstances.[17]

[11]"The Oxford Comparison to the Supreme Court of the United States", edited by Kermitt L. Hall (1992).

[12] Adair v. United States, 208 US 161 (1907), at 175.

[13]Ibid. at 175. (emphasis added)

[14]Ibid. at 191.

[15]Ibid. at 191.

[16]"Supra at Note 10 at 157.

[17]RCW 19.36.010; Lasser v. Grunbaum Bros. Furniture Co., 46 Wn. 2d 402 (1955). DePhilips v. Zolt Const. Co., 136 Wn.2d 26 (1998).

The public policy argument Justice Holmes raised in his dissent has also become an exception to the Employment at Will Doctrine; that being, an employer cannot terminate an employee in violation of public policy.[18]

Many laws have been enacted by Congress and the state legislature which govern the employer/employee relationship, each of which alters the Employment at Will Doctrine in some fashion, and each, as Justice Holmes believed, is allowed by the Constitution.[19] These statutes cover many issues – discrimination,[20] union activity,[21] employee benefits,[22] hours worked,[23] age discrimination,[24] worker safety,[25] civil rights,[26] disability,[27] and veterans' rights.[28]

The Employment at Will Doctrine, which purports to afford employers the right to terminate an employee for any reason or no reason at all;[29]

[18]Thompson v. St. Regis Paper Co., 102 Wn.2d 219 (1984).

[19]Ibid. at Note 11.

[20]42 USC §2000E et seq. and RCW 49.60 et seq.

[21]29 USC §141 et seq. Krystad v. Lau, 65 Wn.2d 827 (1965).

[22] 29 USC §1161 et seq. and RCW 43.72 et seq.

[23] 29 USC §201 et seq. and RCW 49.28.010 et seq.

[24] 29 USC §621 et seq. and RCW 49.44.090.

[25] 29 USC §651 et seq. and RCW 49.17 et seq.

[26] 42 USC §1981 and 1983.

[27] 49 USC §12101, 12213 and RCW 49.60.181(1).

[28] 46 USC §4301 et seq. and RCW 73.16.033.

[29] Gaglidari v. Denny's Restaurants, Inc., 117 W.2d 426 (1991).

does not relieve the employer from the burden of establishing that it did not terminate the employee in violation of the statutes set out above.[30] The initial burden of proof rests with the charging party, who must show that he/she fit into a protected class, was qualified, was doing satisfactory work, and was subjected to an adverse employment action. This has been further defined:

> (1) that plaintiff engaged in an activity protected by Title VII; (2) that the exercise of his [her] civil rights was known by defendant; (3) that, thereafter, the defendant took an employment action adverse to plaintiff; and (4) that there was a causal connection between the protected activity and the adverse employment action.
> Once this has been established, the burden shifts to the employer to show that the reason for the termination was not part of any prohibited activity. The employee must prove by a preponderance of evidence that the reason given by the employer is pretextual, and that the alleged unlawful reason was a substantial factor in the adverse employment action.[31]

Once this has been established, the burden shifts to the employer to show that the reason for the termination was not part of any prohibited activity.[32] The employee must then persuade the court that the reason is pretextual to prevail,[35] that the alleged unlawful reason was a substantial factor in the adverse employment action,[36] and this must be proven with a preponderance of the evidence.[37]

Employers have been meeting this burden for years in the Labor Arbitration arena[38] by establishing mechanisms to show the employee was terminated for performance, lack of work or some other business reason.

JUST CAUSE STANDARD

The time has come for the Washington State Supreme Court to take its lead from the Court in Atlantic Richfield, supra, which stated: "... the future of that doctrine is a compelling issue..." at 898. Well, the future is now. The Court should establish a doctrine other than Employment at Will for the employer/employee relationship in Washington.

[30]Green v. McDonnell Douglas Corp., 411 U.S. 792 (1973).

[31]Hollins v. Atlantis Co., Inc., 188 F.3d 652 (6th Cir. 1999)

[32]Supra Note 30.

[35]Supra Note 30.

[36]MacKay v. Acorn Custom Cabinetry 127 W2nd 302 (1995)

[37]Carle v. McChord Credit Union 65 W2nd 93 (1992)

[38]See generally, Huntington Chair Corp. 24LA490 (1955).

The only equitable standard for terminating an employee is termination for cause. This is not the first time such a standard has been proposed for Washington State.[39] Instituting a termination for cause standard would also establish a consistent model for employers in all termination cases.

Under current law, employers are told that employees can be terminated "for no cause, good cause or even cause morally wrong without fear of liability."[40] This is simply not accurate. An employer's ability to terminate an employee has many restrictions, as discussed previously. Under a just cause standard, an employer would clearly understand its duty.

The burden of proof would be no more problematic than is currently required for any other wrongful discharge case. The Washington Supreme Court has established the burden of proof: "Once the employee has demonstrated that his discharge may have been motivated by reasons that countervene a clear mandate of public policy, the burden shifts to the employer to provide that the dismissal was for reasons other than those alleged by the employee."[41]

An employee would have the burden to establish that he/she was employed by this specific employer and that the employer involuntarily terminated him. Then, the burden would shift to the employer to establish that the basis for the involuntary termination was for cause. This concept is not new--employers covered by a collective bargaining agreement currently have the burden of establishing just cause in termination cases.[42]

The Washington State Supreme Court has defined just cause in the employee discharge context as: ". . . a fair and honest cause or reason regulated by good faith on the part of the party exercising the power. We further hold a discharge for 'just cause' is one that is not for any arbitrary, capricious, or illegal reason and which is based on facts [1] supported by substantial evidence, and [2] reasonably believed by the employer to be true."[43]

In employee discipline situations traditional labor arbitrators have taken the position: "Offenses are of two general classes: (1) those extremely serious offenses such as stealing, striking a foreman, persistent refusal to obey a legitimate order, etc. which usually justifies summary discharge without the necessity of prior warnings or attempts at corrective discipline;

[39]"Penetrating Doctrinal Camouflage: Understanding the Development of the Law of Wrongful Discharge", Cornelius J. Peck, 66 Wa. Law Review, 719.

[40]Supra Note 30 at 226.

[41]Supra Note 30 at 232.

[42]Elkouri and Elkouri, "How Arbitration Works", 3rd Ed. (1979).

[43]Baldwin v. Sisters of Providence, 112 Wn.2d 127, (1989) at 139.

(2) those less serious infractions of plant rules or of proper conduct such as tardiness, absence without permission, careless workmanship, insolence etc., which call not for discharge for the first offense (and usually not even for the second or third offense) but for some milder penalty aimed at correction."[44]

A growing number of employers have established employee policies which outline the relationship between the employer/employee. These employee policies are currently an exception to the Employment at Will Doctrine in that an employer must follow the rules created by such policies when the employee is aware of their existence and they create an expectancy of treatment in accordance with those policies.[45]

The Association for Human Resource Professionals[46] recommends to its members: "Always use progressive discipline. . ."[47] Furthermore: "Workplace disciplinary systems are grounded on the theory of rehabilitation, not punishment."[48] This reveals the position of the professionals in the field of employer/employee relationships.

The courts should establish a strong, yet rebuttable, presumption that when an employer follows a progressive or corrective discipline program, but ultimately terminates an employee for his or her failure to meet the performance requirements outlined in this disciplinary program, the termination is for cause. This presumption should only be rebutted with clear, cogent and convincing evidence[49] (i.e., it is highly probable) that the progressive or corrective discipline was pretextual.

Progressive discipline is when the employer uses successive steps in the corrective process from oral warnings to termination for those "less serious infractions." Generally this will be an oral warning followed by a written warning, then something more substantial – like suspension or termination.[50]

[44]Huntington Chair Corp., 24LA490 at 491 (1955).

[45]DePhillips v. Zolt Const. Co., supra. at note 18.

[46]The Society for Human Resource Management.

[47]Frances T. Coleman, "Cardinal Rules of Termination", (1998).

[48]Ibid.

[49]Colonial Imports V. Carlton Northwest 121 W2nd 726 (1993)

[50]Guardian Industries Corp. v. Grew, 319 NLRB 74 (1995).

Following this recommendation would not preclude an employer from terminating without progressive or corrective discipline in case of extreme employee behavior,[51] or lay-offs for lack of work or other changing economic conditions. This standard would simply mean the employer, if challenged, would have to establish the action met the definition of cause and was not pretextual, for the Employee would be afforded the substantial factor and preponderance of the evidence standard, supra.

CONCLUSION

To the extent there is an Employment at Will Doctrine today, when its many exceptions are taken into consideration, it is clear it would not be recognized by Messieurs Cooley, Blackstone, Wood, or the majority of the 1907 U.S. Supreme Court, which decided Adair, supra, or even the 1928 Washington Supreme Court which decided Davidson, supra.

The doctrine is but a shell of its former self and has no place in the modern employer/employee relationship. The very statutory scheme, i.e. union membership, that the U.S. Supreme Court found unconstitutional in Adair, supra. and on which it based its decision has since been held constitutional.[52]

It seems clear that a sound economy and human dignity are grounded in a stable work force. A human being potentially having his or her livelihood severed by "whim, capriciousness, prejudice or malice"[53] should not be the standard upon which the employer/employee relationship rests as we move into the 21st century.

The time has come for the courts to recognize for all employees what the more progressive employers have implemented -- a just cause standard of termination with a rebuttable presumption favoring progressive or corrective discipline.

[51]Supra, Note 42.

[52]NLRB v. Jones & Laughlin Steel Corp., 301 U.S. 1 (1937).

[53]T.M. Cooley, supra. at note 9.

ETHICAL CONCERNS FOR THE CREDIT MANAGER

By: James H. Hopkins, J.D., S.P.H.R.*

While reviewing past-due accounts, a credit manager notices XYZ Corp. is significantly past-due on a considerably large receivable. As if by telepathy, her phone rings and the controller of XYZ Corp. is on the phone. Taking advantage of this fortuitous opportunity, the credit manager asks the controller when she may expect payment. The controller says that is exactly the reason for her call. She happens to have front row, center stage tickets to a sold out play that evening, and she would like the Credit Manager to join her. She suggests they discuss the account at dinner before the play.

What should the credit manager's answer be? If it were lunch, would the answer be different? If it were golf at a private country club, would that affect the answer? Is price the controlling factor? This is an ethical dilemma which credit managers find themselves exposed to on a regular basis.

Employee Responsibility

Every employee owes their undivided loyalty to their employer. Anything that would interfere with that loyalty is not appropriate behavior. In the hypothetical situation above, the controller may be attempting to influence the credit manager's handling of the past-due account. Over dinner and during the play, the credit manager may be more receptive to give the controller more time to pay. Or the controller may be attempting to lull the credit manager into believing payment will be forthcoming. With this false sense of security, the credit manager may allow lien rights and other forms of security to be lost.

This situation calls for the credit manager to look to her own moral compass for guidance. She will need to determine whether accepting such an invitation would give her employer and/or her subordinates the impression that her loyalties are "for sale." While her decision may be an individual one, the credit manager may also look to her company's guidelines in determining whether this is an appropriate situation or not.
Company Responsibility

Although the contemplation of business ethics is not new – it has been discussed for 2,000 years or more –it has gained attention since the social responsibility movement in the 1960s. At that time, an increasing number of people took the position that because companies were making profits from the country's resources, they were obligated to work to improve the problems of society. A survey taken 20 years later indicates that 76% of corporations now have a code of ethics in place spelling out its values and providing guidelines for its employees.

Because so many decisions in the workplace do not involve a simple "black or white" or "right or wrong" response, it is to the employer's advantage to see that a code of ethics is in place to provide the employees with a clear idea of the company's values and present employees with guidelines for dealing with the wide "gray area" which will be encountered in the world of business ethics.

Often, a company will be well on the road to a code of ethics without realizing it. By incorporating the company's position on issues such as discrimination, dress requirements, illegal drugs, and/or reporting of illegal or questionable activity into its employee handbook or its employment policies, it has already begun laying the groundwork for an ethics code. Larger companies with several departments may decide to develop an individual code for each department, as well as an overall corporate code, to provide applicable guidelines, create a team environment and strengthen its departments.

Instituting a code of ethics will be meaningless unless it is practiced and valued by the company's top personnel. The practice of ethical behavior by a company's employees is definitely enforced through the action of its leaders, not through words alone.

Advance knowledge of behaviors that are valued and those that will not be tolerated, better equip employees to handle ethical dilemmas. It also provides the employer with a measure of protection against litigation by instilling a value system that would discourage illegal behavior (i.e. discrimination in hiring, etc.).

Conclusion

There will certainly be times when socializing over golf, lunch, or even a play with a customer may be appropriate. Socialization or acceptance of gratuities - large or small - must not affect the credit manager's dealings with the customer or in any way put the employer in a compromised position.

* Mr. Hopkins represents business clients in all areas of matters relating to business and commercial transactions, as well as situations relating to the employer/employee relationship. Mr. Hopkins has 20 years' experience assisting business in these areas.

WHEN IT COMES TO CONSTRUCTION LIENS, STRICT COMPLIANCE IS REQUIRED

By: James H. Hopkins JD SPHR

Recently, a Division II of the Washington State Court of Appeals decision once again made clear what those in the construction industry know -- that the Mechanic's and Materialmen's Lien Statute (RCW 60.04, et seq.) is a creation of the state legislature, and thus commands strict compliance. The court's reaffirmation reminds us that a review of the statute's specific requirements is a good idea from time to time.

Notices to owners of real property is one of the requirements suppliers, subcontractors, and general contractors must strictly follow. The three notices most commonly used in the construction industry are the Notice to Customer, Notice to Owner, and Claim of Lien.

NOTICE TO CUSTOMER

Not all notice requirements are found within the Lien Statute. The Contractor's Registration Statute (RCW 18.27.14) requires general contractors who wish to have lien rights provide a Notice to Customer prior to commencing work on a project.

NOTICE TO CUSTOMER

This contractor,
_____
_ is registered with the State of Washington, Registration No. _____, as a general/specialty contractor and has posted with the state a bond or cash deposit of $6,000/$4,000 for the purpose of satisfying claims against the contractor for negligent or improper work or breach of contract in the conduct of the contractor's business. The expiration date of this contractor's registration is _____.
This bond or cash deposit may not be sufficient to cover a claim which might arise from the work done under your contract. If any supplier of materials used in your construction project or any employee of the contractor or subcontractor is not paid by the contractor or sub contractor on your job, your property may be liened to force payment. If you wish additional protection, you may request the contractor to provide you with original "lien release" documents from each supplier or subcontractor on your project. The contractor is required to provide you with further information about lien release documents if you request it. General information is also available from the Department of Labor of Industries.

NOTICE TO OWNER

Those professionals and material and equipment suppliers who do not have a contractual relationship directly with the owner of the real property, must provide a Notice to Owner. Second-tier or lower subcontractors must also give this notice. A Notice to Owner must be provided within 60 days of the first work or delivery on commercial projects and within 10 days of first work or delivery on residential construction projects.

NOTICE TO OWNER

IMPORTANT: READ BOTH SIDES OF THIS NOTICE CAREFULLY.

PROTECT YOURSELF FROM PAYING TWICE

     To:
     Date:
     Re: (description of property: Street address or general location.)
     From:

     AT THE REQUEST OF: (Name of person ordering the professional services, materials, or equipment.

     THIS IS NOT A LIEN: This notice is sent to you to tell you who is providing professional services, materials, or equipment for the improvement of your property and to advise you of the rights of these persons and your responsibilities. Also take note that laborers on your project may claim a lien without sending you a notice.

OWNER/OCCUPIER OF EXISTING RESIDENTIAL PROPERTY

Under Washington law, those who furnish labor, professional services, materials, or equipment for the repair, remodel, or alteration of your owner-occupied principal residence and who are not paid, have a right to enforce their claim for payment against your property. This claim is known as a construction lien.

The law limits the amount that a lien claimant can claim against your property. Claims may only be made against that portion of the contract price you have not yet paid to your prime contractor as of the time this notice was given to you or three days after this notice was mailed to you. Review the back of this notice for more information and ways to avoid lien claims.

COMMERCIAL AND/OR NEW RESIDENTIAL PROPERTY

We have or will be providing professional services, materials, or equipment for the improvement of your commercial or new residential project. In the event you or your contractor fail to pay us, we may file a lien against your property. A lien may be claimed for all professional services, materials, or equipment furnished after a date that is sixty days before this notice was given to you or mailed to you, unless the improvement to your property is the construction of a new single-family residence, then ten days before this notice was given to you or mailed to you.

Sender:

Address:

Telephone:

Brief description of professional services, materials, or equipment provided or to be provided: _____
_____
_____.

IMPORTANT INFORMATION FOR YOUR PROTECTION

This notice is sent to inform you that we have or will provide professional services, materials, or equipment for the improvement of your property. We expect to be paid by the person who ordered our services, but if we are not paid, we have the right to enforce our claim by filing a construction lien against your property.

LEARN more about the lien laws and the meaning of this notice by discussing them with your contractor, suppliers, Department of Labor and Industries, the firm sending you this Notice, your lender, or your attorney.

COMMON METHODS TO AVOID CONSTRUCTION LIENS: There are several methods available to protect your property from construction liens. The following are two of the more commonly used methods.

DUAL PAYCHECKS (Joint Checks): When paying your contractor for services or materials, you may make checks payable jointly to the contractor and the firms furnishing you this notice.

LIEN RELEASES: You may require your contractor to provide lien releases signed by all the suppliers and subcontractors from whom you have received this notice. If they cannot obtain lien releases because you have not paid them, you may use the dual payee check method to protect yourself.

YOU SHOULD TAKE APPROPRIATE STEPS TO PROTECT YOUR PROPERTY FROM LIENS.

YOUR PRIME CONTRACTOR AND YOUR CONSTRUCTION LENDER ARE REQUIRED BY LAW TO GIVE YOU WRITTEN INFORMATION ABOUT LIEN CLAIMS. IF YOU HAVE NOT RECEIVED IT, ASK THEM FOR IT.

cc: Prime Contractor
Certified Mail #_____

Return Receipt Requested

CLAIM OF LIEN

A lien is created against the real property when a Claim of Lien is properly recorded. A properly recorded lien is one that as been recorded with the county auditor in the county where the property is located. The county auditor will also require that a cover sheet be provided. The individual or entity wishing to secure a lien must record the lien within 90 days of the last work or delivery on the project.

Within 14 days of recording, a copy of the lien must be mailed by registered or certified mail or by personal service to the owner or the lien claimant will not have a claim for attorney's fees.

After recording return to:
_____ [claimant]
_____
_____ [address]

CLAIM OF LIEN

_____
_____, Claimant vs.
(name of person indebted to claimant)

Notice is hereby given that the person named below claims a lien pursuant to chapter 60.04 RCW. In support of this lien the following information is submitted:

1. NAME OF LIEN CLAIMANT:

   TELEPHONE NUMBER:
   ADDRESS:

2. DATE ON WHICH THE CLAIMANT BEGAN TO PERFORM LABOR, PROVIDE PROFESSIONAL SERVICES, SUPPLY MATERIAL OR EQUIPMENT OR DATE ON WHICH EMPLOYEE BENEFIT CONTRIBUTIONS BECAME DUE:

3. NAME OF PERSON INDEBTED TO THE CLAIMANT:

4. DESCRIPTION OF THE PROPERTY AGAINST WHICH A LIEN ISCLAIMED (street address, legal description or other information that will reasonably describe the property):

5. NAME OF THE OWNER OR REPUTED OWNER (If not known state "unknown"):

6. THE LAST DATE ON WHICH LABOR WAS PERFORMED; PROFESSIONAL SERVICES WERE FURNISHED; CONTRIBUTIONS TO AN EMPLOYEE BENEFIT PLAN WERE DUE: OR MATERIAL, OR EQUIPMENT WAS FURNISHED:

7. PRINCIPAL AMOUNT FOR WHICH THE LIEN IS CLAIMED:

8. IF THE CLAIMANT IS THE ASSIGNEE OF THIS CLAIM SO STATE HERE:

_____,
Claimant

(Phone number, address, city and state of claimant)

STATE OF WASHINGTON)
) SS.
COUNTY OF   )

_____,
being sworn, says: I am the claimant (or attorney of the claimant, or administrator, representative, or agent of the trustees of an employee benefit plan) above-named; I have read or heard the foregoing claim, read and know the contents thereof, and believe the same to be true and correct and that the claim of lien is not frivolous and is made with reasonable cause, and is not clearly excessive under penalty of perjury.

_____

_____

I certify that I know or have satisfactory evidence that _____ is the person who appeared before me, and said person acknowledged that _____ signed this instrument and acknowledged it to be _____ free and voluntary act for the uses and purposes mentioned in the instrument.

Dated: _____

_____

NOTARY PUBLIC in and for the State of Washington, Residing at
_____
My Commission expires: _____

cc: Owner   Certified mail #_____
             Return receipt requested

cc: Prime Contractor   Certified mail #_____
             Return receipt requested

cc: Claimant's Customer   Certified mail #_____
    (if other than owner   Return receipt requested
     or prime contractor)

The lien claimant or a representative must verify that the lien is "just." Failure to do so will invalidate the lien. In addition, the Claim of Lien must include the legal description or address, which is reasonably calculated to identify the piece of property.

Whether attempting to enforce a lien or defend against one, knowing that each lien must comply with the statute which created it is a valuable piece of information. Parties to any construction contract, like all contracts, need to take steps to ensure they will be compensated for their efforts. Relying upon the Lien Statutes for payment may not be the best way, especially if care is not followed in preparing the lien documents. In conjunction with a sound credit policy, proper use of the Lien Statute can be helpful in getting paid for work performed.

MECHANIC'S AND MATERIALMAN'S LIENS IN WASHINGTON

By: James H. Hopkins JD SPHR

Credit Managers have many ways to assist them in collecting the money owed their respective companies and just one of those is the mechanic and materialman lien statutes in their states on construction projects. The Courts have consistently held as these statutes are created by state legislatures strict compliance is a necessity. This article reviews those requirements in Washington State.

The notices to the owner of real property is one of the requirements suppliers, subcontractors, and general contractors must strictly follow. The three notices required are the Notice to Customer, Notice to Owner, and Claim of Lien.

NOTICE TO CUSTOMER

Not all notice requirements are found within the Lien Statute. The Contractor's Registration Statute (RCW 18.27.14) requires general contractors who wish to have lien rights to provide a Notice to Customer prior to commencing work on a project.

NOTICE TO CUSTOMER

This contractor,
_____

_ is registered with the State of Washington, Registration No. _____, as a general/specialty contractor and has posted with the state a bond or cash deposit of $6,000/$4,000 for the purpose of satisfying claims against the contractor for negligent or improper work or breach of contract in the conduct of the contractor's business. The expiration date of this contractor's registration is _____.
This bond or cash deposit may not be sufficient to cover a claim, which might arise from the work done under your contract. If any supplier of materials used in your construction project or any employee of the contractor or subcontractor is not paid by the contractor or sub contractor on your job, your property may be liened to force payment. If you wish additional protection, you may request the contractor to provide you with original "lien release" documents from each supplier or subcontractor on your project. The contractor is required to provide you with further information about lien release documents if you request it. General information is also available from the Department of Labor of Industries.

NOTICE TO OWNER

Those professionals and material and equipment suppliers, who do not have a contractual relationship directly with the owner of the real property, must provide a Notice to Owner. Second-tier or lower subcontractors must also give this notice. A Notice to Owner must be provided within 60 days of the first work or delivery on commercial projects and within 10 days of first work or delivery on residential construction projects.

NOTICE TO OWNER

IMPORTANT: READ BOTH SIDES OF THIS NOTICE CAREFULLY.

PROTECT YOURSELF FROM PAYING TWICE

To:
Date:
Re: (description of property: Street address or general location.)
From:

AT THE REQUEST OF: (Name of person ordering the professional services, materials, or equipment.

THIS IS NOT A LIEN: This notice is sent to you to tell you who is providing professional services, materials, or equipment for the improvement of your property and to advise you of the rights of these persons and your responsibilities. Also take note that laborers on your project may claim a lien without sending you a notice.

OWNER/OCCUPIER OF EXISTING RESIDENTIAL PROPERTY

Under Washington law, those who furnish labor, professional services, materials, or equipment for the repair, remodel, or alteration of your owner-occupied principal residence and who are not paid, have a right to enforce their claim for payment against your property. This claim is known as a construction lien.

The law limits the amount that a lien claimant can claim against your property. Claims may only be made against that portion of the contract price you have not yet paid to your prime contractor as of the time this notice was given to you or three days after this notice was mailed to you. Review the back of this notice for more information and ways to avoid lien claims.

COMMERCIAL AND/OR NEW RESIDENTIAL PROPERTY

We have or will be providing professional services, materials, or equipment for the improvement of your commercial or new residential project. In the event you or your contractor fail to pay us, we may file a lien against your property. A lien may be claimed for all professional services, materials, or equipment furnished after a date that is sixty days before this notice was given to you or mailed to you, unless the improvement to your property is the construction of a new single-family residence, then ten days before this notice was given to you or mailed to you.

Sender:

Address:

Telephone:

Brief description of professional services, materials, or equipment provided or to be provided: _____
_____
_____.

IMPORTANT INFORMATION FOR YOUR PROTECTION

This notice is sent to inform you that we have or will provide professional services, materials, or equipment for the improvement of your property. We expect to be paid by the person who ordered our services, but if we are not paid, we have the right to enforce our claim by filing a construction lien against your property.

LEARN more about the lien laws and the meaning of this notice by discussing them with your contractor, suppliers, Department of Labor and Industries, the firm sending you this Notice, your lender, or your attorney.

COMMON METHODS TO AVOID CONSTRUCTION LIENS: There are several methods available to protect your property from construction liens. The following are two of the more commonly used methods.

DUAL PAYCHECKS (Joint Checks): When paying your contractor for services or materials, you may make checks payable jointly to the contractor and the firms furnishing you this notice.

LIEN RELEASES: You may require your contractor to provide lien releases signed by all the suppliers and subcontractors from whom you have received this notice. If they cannot obtain lien releases because you have not paid them, you may use the dual payee check method to protect yourself.

YOU SHOULD TAKE APPROPRIATE STEPS TO PROTECT YOUR PROPERTY FROM LIENS.

YOUR PRIME CONTRACTOR AND YOUR CONSTRUCTION LENDER ARE REQUIRED BY LAW TO GIVE YOU WRITTEN INFORMATION ABOUT LIEN CLAIMS. IF YOU HAVE NOT RECEIVED IT, ASK THEM FOR IT.

cc: Prime Contractor
Certified Mail #_____

Return Receipt Requested

CLAIM OF LIEN

A lien is created against the real property when a Claim of Lien is properly recorded. A properly recorded lien is one that as been recorded with the county auditor in the county where the property is located. The county auditor will also require that a cover sheet be provided. The individual or entity wishing to secure a lien must record the lien within 90 days of the last work or delivery on the project.

Within 14 days of recording, a copy of the lien must be mailed by registered or certified mail or by personal service to the owner or the lien claimant will not have a claim for attorney's fees.

After recording return to:
_____ [Claimant]
_____
_____ [Address]

CLAIM OF LIEN

_____
_____, Claimant vs.
(name of person indebted to claimant)

Notice is hereby given that the person named below claims a lien pursuant to chapter 60.04 RCW. In support of this lien the following information is submitted:

1. NAME OF LIEN CLAIMANT:

   TELEPHONE NUMBER:
   ADDRESS:

2. DATE ON WHICH THE CLAIMANT BEGAN TO PERFORM LABOR, PROVIDE PROFESSIONAL SERVICES, SUPPLY MATERIAL OR EQUIPMENT OR DATE ON WHICH EMPLOYEE BENEFIT CONTRIBUTIONS BECAME DUE:

3. NAME OF PERSON INDEBTED TO THE CLAIMANT:

4. DESCRIPTION OF THE PROPERTY AGAINST WHICH A LIEN ISCLAIMED (Street address, legal description or other information that will reasonably describe the property):

5. NAME OF THE OWNER OR REPUTED OWNER (If not known state "unknown"):

6. THE LAST DATE ON WHICH LABOR WAS PERFORMED; PROFESSIONAL SERVICES WERE FURNISHED; CONTRIBUTIONS TO AN EMPLOYEE BENEFIT PLAN WERE DUE: OR MATERIAL, OR EQUIPMENT WAS FURNISHED:

7. PRINCIPAL AMOUNT FOR WHICH THE LIEN IS CLAIMED:

8. IF THE CLAIMANT IS THE ASSIGNEE OF THIS CLAIM SO STATE HERE:

_____,
Claimant

_____
(Phone number, address, city and state of claimant)

STATE OF WASHINGTON)
) S.
COUNTY OF   )

_____,
Being sworn, says: I am the claimant (or attorney of the claimant, or administrator, representative, or agent of the trustees of an employee benefit plan) above-named; I have read or heard the foregoing claim, read and know the contents thereof, and believe the same to be true and correct and that the claim of lien is not frivolous and is made with reasonable cause, and is not clearly excessive under penalty of perjury.

_____

I certify that I know or have satisfactory evidence that _____ is the person who appeared before me, and said person acknowledged that _____ signed this instrument and acknowledged it to be _____ free and voluntary act for the uses and purposes mentioned in the instrument.

    Dated: _____

_____
NOTARY PUBLIC in and for the State of Washington, Residing at
_____
My Commission expires: _____

cc: Owner   Certified mail #_____
        Return receipt requested

cc: Prime Contractor Certified mail #_____
        Return receipt requested

cc: Claimant's Customer   Certified mail #_____
    (If other than owner   Return receipt requested
      Or prime contractor)

The lien claimant or a representative must verify that the lien is "just." Failure to do so will invalidate the lien. In addition, the Claim of Lien must include the legal description or address, which is reasonably calculated to identify the piece of property.

Whether attempting to enforce a lien or defend against one, knowing that each lien must comply with the statute, which created it, is a valuable piece of information. Parties to any construction contract, like all contracts, need to take steps to ensure they will be compensated for their efforts. Relying upon the Lien Statutes for payment may not be the best way, especially if care is not followed in preparing the lien documents. In conjunction with a sound credit policy, proper use of the Lien Statute can be helpful in getting paid for work performed.

USING THE MILLER ACT TO COLLECT ON FEDERAL PROJECTS

By: James H. Hopkins JD SPHR

Whenever a federal public project calls for construction, alteration or repair in excess of $25,000, the prime contractor is required to furnish a payment bond pursuant to the "Miller Act". This payment bond is separate from and in addition to the performance bond that a prime contractor must provide for the benefit of the U.S. Government.

Determining the Bond Amount

When the prime contract is for less than $1 million dollars, the amount of the bond must be 50% of the contract amount. When the prime contract is for an amount between $1 million dollars and $5 million dollars, the bond must be for 40% of the contract amount. When the contract is for an amount greater than $5 million dollars, the required bond must be $2.5 million dollars.

As one can clearly see, in the event that multiple parties claim against the bond on a prime contract, which has serious problems, there is little security against a loss.

Parties Protected by the Bond

The Miller Act provides coverage to either persons or firms involved in the construction, alteration or repair of any federal project who have a direct contractual relationship with either the prime contractor (first-tier claimants), or subcontractors who in turn have a direct contractual relationship with the prime contractor (second-tier claimants).

Notice Requirements

Any subcontractor, supplier, or laborer who does not have a direct contractual relationship with the contractor (second-tier claimants) must give written notice to the prime contractor within 90 days of the last day of furnishing labor or materials.

The required notice must state with substantial accuracy the amount claimed, the name of the subcontractor, and to whom the labor or material was furnished. A sample of the notice is outlined below:

TO: (prime contractor)

You are hereby notified that the undersigned claimant has furnished (labor, materials, supplies or equipment) for use in the prosecution of the work of (public agency, contract number) at the request of (name of subcontractor). The last day of furnishing (labor, materials, supplies or equipment) was _____. The undersigned makes claim against you and your surety for payment of $_____ which sum is due and owing to the undersigned.

      DATED this _____ day of _____, 199__.

Name of Claimant
Address
Phone Number

Signature
Title
Contractor Registration Number

      This notice must be mailed to the contractor by registered mail, postage prepaid, or personally served by the U.S. Marshall.

      The statute is very clear that these are the only ways in which this notice may be provided. Any deviation in service could be fatal to a claim.

      Inspection of work already performed or correction of defective work by a potential claimant will not extend the time period for providing the notice

Foreclosure

The lawsuit against a Miller Act bond -- which is called a foreclosure action – must be commenced within one (1) year from the date of last furnishing labor or material to the project. As discussed previously, neither inspection of work already performed nor correction of defective work will extend this time period.

The action for foreclosure on a Miller Act bond must be brought in the United States District Court in the district where the project is located.

After Winning, What Do You Receive

There is no provision in the Miller Act for an award of attorneys' fees to a successful claimant in a foreclosure action. When the underlying contract between the claimant and its customer has a provision for attorneys' fees, the court may award them to the successful party.

Interest on the amount of claim may be allowed commencing with the date payment was due from the debtor.

Both the awarding of interest and attorneys' fees is at the discretion of the court hearing the foreclosure action.

As discussed previously, the bond provided pursuant to the Miller Act is not for 100% of the project. Therefore, in the event the claims exceed the face value of the bond; the claimants will receive a pro rata share of the bond proceeds.

Conclusion

It should be clear at this point that although a Miller Act bond is provided on a federal project and affords some protection to those providing labor and/or materials, it should in no way be a substitute for a good, sound credit policy.

This Article has been provided by James H. Hopkins.

REVISITING THE MILLER ACT: COLLECTIONS ON FEDERAL PROJECTS

By: James H. Hopkins JD SPHR

An article entitled "Using the Miller Act to Collect on Federal Projects" appeared in this publication in November 1998. On August 17, 1999, Congress amended Title 40 U.S. Code Sections 270a and 270b, known as the Miller Act. The current amendments warrant a revisit of this issue.

Congress left unchanged the requirement that prime contractors on Federal Public Projects furnish a payment bond for construction, alteration or repairs in excess of $25,000. The prime contractor must also continue to post a separate performance bond for the benefit of the U.S. Government.

Determining the Bond Amount

One area of the Miller Act that Congress did change is the dollar amount of the bond required of prime contractors.

Previously, on a prime contract of less than $1 million dollars, the amount of the bond was 50% of the contract amount. On prime contract between $1 million dollars and $5 million dollars, the bond was 40% of the contract amount. Contracts in excess of $5 million dollars required a bond of $2.5 million dollars.

With the latest amendments, the amount of the bond is simply calculated as 100% of the "total amount payable by the terms of the contract." However, if the contracting officer determines that such an amount is impractical, he or she can set the amount of the bond.

This change will likely have a positive effect on losses when multiple parties claim against the bond on a prime contract with serious problems. Now there may be enough money in the bond to pay all of the claims.

Parties Protected by the Bond

The parties covered by the Miller Act remain the same: persons or firms involved in the construction, alteration or repair of any federal project who have a direct contractual relationship with either the prime contractor (first-tier claimants), or subcontractors who in turn have a direct contractual relationship with the prime contractor (second-tier claimants) are protected.

Notice Requirements

The notice requirements remain the same: any subcontractor, supplier, or laborer who does not have a direct contractual relationship with the contractor (second-tier claimants) must give written notice to the prime contractor within 90 days of the last day of furnishing labor or materials. This provision did not change with the last amendments.

The required form of notice still must state with substantial accuracy the amount claimed, the name of the subcontractor, and to whom the labor or material was furnished. A sample of the notice is outlined below:

TO: (prime contractor)

You are hereby notified that the undersigned claimant has furnished (labor, materials, supplies or equipment) for use in the prosecution of the work of (public agency, contract number) at the request of (name of subcontractor). The last day of furnishing (labor, materials, supplies or equipment) was _____. The undersigned makes claim against you and your surety for payment of $_____ which sum is due and owing to the undersigned.

DATED this _____ day of _____, 199__.

Name of Claimant
Address
Phone Number

Signature
Title
Contractor Registration Number

    The statute used to be very specific in how notice was to be given, and any deviation in service was potentially fatal to a claim. With Congress' passage of Public Law 106-49, the language regarding how notices are to be provided was amended to read "any means which provides written third-party verification of delivery." The Code Revisor has taken the position that this section "could not be executed. . ." What this all means is a mystery.

    As the status of the amendment on this issue is unclear, it is recommended that claimants continue to follow the pre-amendment requirement that the notice must be mailed to the contractor by registered mail, postage prepaid, or personally served by the U.S. Marshall. In the event the amendment is not valid, serving notice in another fashion may prove fatal; however, should the new language be adopted, nothing would be lost by following the pre-amendment rule.

Inspection of work already performed or correction of defective work by a potential claimant will not extend the time period for providing the notice.

Foreclosure

No changes were made to the commencement of commencement of a lawsuit against a Miller Act bond – also known as a foreclosure action. Such an action must be commenced within one (1) year from the date of last furnishing labor or material to the project. As discussed previously, neither inspection of work already performed nor correction of defective work will extend this time period.

The action for foreclosure on a Miller Act bond must be brought in the United States District Court in the district where the project is located.

After Winning, What Do You Receive

There is no provision in the Miller Act for an award of attorneys' fees to a successful claimant in a foreclosure action. When the underlying contract between the claimant and its customer has a provision for attorneys' fees, the court may award them to the successful party.

Interest on the amount of claim may be allowed commencing with the date payment was due from the debtor.

Both the awarding of interest and attorneys' fees is at the discretion of the court hearing the foreclosure action.

Conclusion

While a Miller Act bond will likely now cover 100% of the project amount on a federal project, affording better protection than before to those providing labor and/or materials, it still is not a substitute for a good, sound credit policy.

This Article has been provided by James H. Hopkins.

NEGOTIATIONS AND THE CREDIT PROFESSIONAL

By: James H. Hopkins, JD SPHR

Credit professionals constantly find themselves in a variety of situations requiring negotiating skills. These situations may include dealing with sales professionals within one's own organization who wish to sell products, customers with less than stellar credit, and/or those with past due accounts.

The Constants in Negotiating

The negotiation process will follow a predictable pattern, regardless of who is taking part in the process. The steps which make up the process are: (1) preparation; (2) initial meeting; (3) recess; and (4) follow up meeting(s).

A. Preparation

A thorough preparation is the key to successful negotiations. Until all parties have invested the time and effort in fully preparing themselves, face-to-face negotiations are not practical.

The first step in preparing for negotiations is to conduct an objective fact-finding to determine the who, what, when and why of the negotiations. Who: Those individuals on both sides of the negotiations who will be critical to reaching an agreement must be identified. While the personalities of the participants should not play a part, in reality, it is difficult to remove this aspect from the process. Therefore, it may be necessary to incorporate the participants' personalities into the fact-finding mission.

What: The negotiator must have a clear understanding of the subject matter of the negotiations. The strengths and weaknesses of your team and the other team need to be identified. For example, a credit professional must be aware of a customer's ability to pay, the strengths or weaknesses of the customer's industry, and the overall strength of the economy.

When: The time frame in which the negotiations must commence and/or be completed should be specified. If no firm time frame applies, it is still a good idea to establish a time line to keep the process on track and moving forward at a reasonable pace.

Why: Both the desired results and the justification of the results should be well-known and clearly identified. The ultimate purpose of the negotiations should not be to crush that so-and-so, but to accomplish an economic result.

By answering these questions, one determines the goals for the negotiations in a rational, logical manner.

While establishing your team's goals, the minimal acceptable position and a maximum expected position are set. The other party to the negotiations will be contemplating their range as well. Where these ranges overlap will determine the settlement range

B.   The Initial Negotiation Meeting

When the preparation process is complete, it is time to commence the actual negotiations. During the initial meeting, the negotiators will put their position on the table, make a general statement as to why they believe their position is just, and verify the information developed during the preparation phase. The amount of information provided to the other side at this time will depend upon many factors -- such as the number of anticipated "follow up" meetings that will take place, the relationship between the negotiators and the overall feeling of the negotiators on how the meeting is going.
At this point, it is important that the parties establish a civil working environment, check egos at the door, and come in with the understanding that the best end result may not make everyone happy, but is one that will be fair to all involved. If a negotiator appears completely inflexible during this "first date", it may signal the collapse of the negotiations and ensure that there will not be a "second date".

If future meetings are to be held, the negotiators should determine where and when these would be held. It is not uncommon for each side to try hold the meeting(s) in a location designed to give them a "home court" advantage. This advantage may mean meeting at the office of one of the negotiators. To eliminate a possible home court advantage for either party, there may be a benefit to holding the negotiations at a neutral site. The major factor in determining whether this is feasible is the costs associated with a neutral location, and whether the parties are willing to come to an agreement about the division of such costs. Care must be taken not to let this become a core issue of negotiations. Some may recall the Paris Peace Talks in the 1970s where the American and Vietnamese negotiators spent days attempting to resolve conflicts over the shape of the negotiating table. Don't let this happen to you! Preparedness will go a long way toward neutralizing any home court advantage the other side may have.

By listening carefully and through thorough preparation, a negotiator will identify early those items the other side appears to deem important, but which are not an issue to the negotiator's position. Doing so will allow the negotiator to quickly make concessions which will communicate flexibility to the other side, without core issues being affected; thereby building goodwill with the other side. Establishing this relationship early by conceding non-issues may prove to be vital later in the negotiations. The other team may be more willing to concede your major points if they feel you have been more than fair.

C. Recess

The parties should recess after this initial meeting and evaluate the information received as well as their respective position. Such a recess may range from a few minutes to a few days. The time frame set out in the preparation phase may dictate how short a recess should be. Another factor in determining the length of the recess is how long it will take for both sides to digest the information provided and to incorporate this information with the information set forth in the preparation phase.

During this time, the settlement range may be narrowed based upon the give and take explored during the initial meeting.

D. Follow Up Meetings

Depending upon one's strengths and/or weakness an overall bargaining strategy and bargaining style will begin to emerge. This strategy and style will set the tone for any future meetings.

The strategy may be to settle early for less dollars or negotiate --taking a tougher position in an attempt to move higher in the settlement range. Again, keep in mind the goals first established and continue working on separating the people from the issues.

Negotiating styles will depend upon the relationship a negotiator has established with the other side. The style may be affected by prior negotiations between the parties, and/or whether the parties' relationship will continue beyond a particular negotiation or whether this is a one-time transaction.

In the event of a one-time transaction, the style may be firmer, with the negotiator continuing to push the initiative and make little or no concessions. On the other hand, if the relationship must continue beyond these negotiations, a more collaborative approach is sensible.

Conclusion

A good negotiator will focus on being positive during the negotiations, being a good listener, and at all times being considerate of the individuals with whom she/he is negotiating.

Use of objective criteria during negotiation and keeping options open to create mutual gain will generally lead to a satisfactory result.

THE NATIONAL LABOR RELATIONS ACT AND NON-UNION EMPLOYERS

By: James H. Hopkins JD SPHR

Employers understand the National Labor Relations Act (NLRA) applies when an employer is dealing with its unionized employees. They also understand that when employees, the NLRA governs union organizing activity. This is when two or more employees of the same employer band together to for better wages, hours or working conditions. The National Labor Relations Board (NLRB) is the administrative agency charged with enforcing the NLRA.

The NLRA prohibits any employer from taking any action to restrain, coerce or interfere with an employee's right to join or refrain from joining or voting for a union.

The U.S. Supreme Court, several Circuit Courts of Appeal, and the NLRB have found violations of the NLRA in situations not identified above.

The NLRB and the Courts have found a violation of the NLRA when an employee was disciplined for criticizing management during a company meeting called by management to announce a change in its break policy. The

NLRB found concerted activity could be inferred from the circumstances, even though no union organizing was present. They reasoned the fact the employee spoke up in front of other employees and was disciplined would have a chilling effect on other employees who may want to organize into a union. In upholding the NLRB's decision, the Court stated, "The employee's questions were concerted activity not merely because they were made at an employee meeting called by the employer, but because they were directed at an announced change in the terms and conditions of employment, the break policy." This seems to imply that disciplining an employee who openly challenges his/her employer in this manner would be considered a violation of the NLRA, regardless of the setting.

The U.S. Supreme Court has ruled that in a union environment when a union member is involved in any disciplinary discussions with their employer, they are entitled to have a union representative present. The NLRB recently ruled this also applies to nonunion employers. A nonunion employee may have another employee present during a meeting where the employee's performance and possible discipline is discussed.

The Courts have also ruled that a blanket prohibition against discussing one's wages with other employees is a violation of the NLRA. The Court stated, " A rule prohibiting employees from communicating with one another regarding wages, a key objective of organizational activity, undoubtedly tends to interfere with the employees' right to engage in protected concerted activity." Once again, this applies whether or not a union is present.

In addition, "cyber communication" (i.e., e-mail) has come under scrutiny by the NLRB. Even though Courts have consistently held that "mere talk" is protected under the NLRA only when it is attempting to motivate "group action", the NLRB has interpreted this to mean that the group action need not be overt. With that in mind, the NLRB has ruled that individual communications on a company's e-mail network can be concerted activity. The specific situation involved management of a non-union employer who sent an e-mail announcing a new compensation package. An employee who objected to the new package responded via e-mail, and when others asked questions of the first employee, he responded. The company disciplined the individual, and the NLRB found a violation of the NLRA. The NLRB felt this was leading to group activity even though there was nothing the employee communicated that would indicate such an intention.

One of the more difficult areas for a nonunion employer, is the employee/management committee. In certain circumstances, federal and state regulations require an employer to have employee/employer committees, which is generally found in the area of safety. The NLRB has looked to see if such committees fit the definition of a "labor organization". The legal definition of a labor organization is "any organization, labor union association, corporation, or society of any kind in which employees participate to any degree whatsoever and which exists for the purpose of dealing with employers concerning grievances, labor disputes, wages, rates of pay or hours of employment." When a committee is found to fit within this definition, it can be looked upon as an employer dominated union, which is a violation of the NLRA. The NLRB has ruled that in order for any employee committee not to violate the NLRA, it can only make proposals and simply gather information, but cannot make recommendations (this is collective bargaining) and cannot act on the information gathered. The NLRB has specifically stated "…the protection of section 7 (NLRA) does not vary depending on whether or not the employees involved are represented by a union, or whether the conduct involved is related, directly or indirectly, to union activity or collective bargaining."

      Staying in compliance with the NLRA and certain administrative codes, which require safety committees, is a daily challenge for any nonunion employer.

Every employer must stay vigilant to any action that could be considered stifling to their employees' concerted activity.

Managers in a nonunion company must be as cognizent of the NLRA as any manager in a union environment.

TIMELY PAYMENT ON CONSTRUCTION PROJECTS

By: James H. Hopkins, J.D. SPHR

On all construction projects, receiving timely payment is one of the highest priorities. It is irrelevant where you fit in the hierarchy of a project -- general contractor to supplier to a sub-subcontractor – receiving prompt payment for materials provided or work completed is a must if you intend to stay in business.

In general, many contractors hold the belief that payment is required no later than 30 days after the work is completed or after an invoice for the work is received. This may in fact be the case, but on a construction project, it may very well be the exception rather than the rule.

Two possible impediments to payment under this belief may be found in the construction contract itself and/or in the statute governing public works projects.

Pay When Pay Contract Clauses

It is becoming the prevailing practice for construction contracts to incorporate "pay when pay" clauses into the terms and conditions on both public works and private projects. Simply stated, pay when pay clauses allow a general contractor or a subcontractor to pay lower-tier subcontractors and suppliers only after payment is received from the party with whom they are contracting.

The Washington courts have held that clauses providing for payment after payment is received are enforceable. Amilco Electric v. Donald M. Drake Co. A clause will be enforced if drafted in such a way that receipt of payment by one party is a condition precedent to entitlement to payment by the other party to the contract. If the language is contradictory to this, the courts will likely say the withholding of payment can only be for a reasonable time.

The incorporation of "pay when pay" clauses in a contract can impede prompt payment, through no fault of a subcontractor or supplier, simply because their customer (the general contractor) has not been paid.

Clearly, the existence of this clause in a construction contract can be viewed favorably by the general contractor, but lower-tier contractors may find this clause to be a hindrance to prompt payment.

Adoption of Prompt Pay Statute on Public Works Contracts

On public works projects, the Washington State legislature has adopted, for want of a better term, a prompt pay statute (RCW 39.04.250). The intent is to ensure that payment be made by the general contractor to lower tiered contractors in a timely fashion by requiring that payments be made by the general contractor to its subcontractors within 10-days of receipt of payment. The subcontractors must then pay their sub-subcontractors within 10-days of being paid, and so forth on down the line.

While the statute speaks of contractors and subcontractors, it is silent as to the rights of suppliers in this prompt pay scenario. No case law is yet on record to interpret this statute in one way or the other; but it is supposed that suppliers of materials would not be able to avail themselves to the protection of this statute on public works projects.

As with the pay when pay clause, the general and upper-tier subcontractors may find the statute to their advantage, but lower-tier contractors most likely would not.

Lower-tier subcontractors may find that the statute provides some measure of assistance to them if a "good faith dispute" exists regarding the right to receive payment. In that scenario, the party owing the payment can withhold no more than 150% of the disputed amount, but must pay any undisputed balance to the lower-tier subcontractors.

Furthermore, contractors who must seek legal recourse to enforce any provision of the statute are entitled to interest and attorney fees. However, since most contracts already build an attorney fees clause into their terms and conditions, the threat of fees and costs under the statute are not likely to ensure greater compliance than the contract terms and conditions themselves.

All things considered, this statute may be viewed as a valuable legal resource by some in the construction industry, but an equal number may find it completely non-beneficial or an actual impediment to prompt payment.

Conclusion

As in most business transactions, the probability of payment is improved when you: (1) know with whom you are doing business; (2) understand the terms and conditions of the contract before agreeing to them; and (3) take all necessary steps to perfect any and all lien rights.

Awareness of the statute and contract clauses affecting timing of payments also places one at an advantage over those who might forecast their accounts receivables too optimistically.

SUCCESSFULLY PROSECUTING CONSTRUCTION CLAIMS BEFORE DISPUTES ARISE

By: James H. Hopkins, JD SPHR

All parties involved in a construction project have expectations that the project will proceed smoothly. However, in reality, claims for extra work or extensions of time often arise. Contractors and/or Subcontractors will enjoy greater success in prosecuting the merits of any extra work or time extension claims if they are knowledgeable about the contract language governing such disputes. This knowledge should be acquired prior to signing any contract --before the project commences, not when the problem arises.

Construction contracts will generally contain language which requires any party making a claim to give notice to the other party within a specified time.

An example of this language can be found in AIA Document A201-1997, which is commonly used in contracts between the General Contractor and the Owner of a project. In paragraph 4.3.1, it states:

Claims by either party must be initiated within 21 days of occurrence of the event giving rise to such claim or within 21 days after the claimant first recognizes the condition giving rise to the claim.

Clearly, making the Notice of Claim within the specified time period is the first step in the process of making any claim under a construction contract containing such language.

Subcontracts or Sub-subcontractors must be aware that many of their contracts will have language incorporating the Terms and Conditions of the General Contractor's contract with the Owner. Lower-tier contractors who sign contracts incorporating the Terms and Conditions of the contract between the General Contractor and the project Owner will find themselves bound by the language contained in the contract -- whether or not they reviewed it before signing.

Below is an example of language that may be found in a contract incorporating the Terms and Conditions of a General Contract:

Subcontract documents include the contract between the owner and general contract, which is incorporated herein and made a part hereof by this reference thereto.

Such an incorporation by reference has been held enforceable by the Washington courts. In Sime Construction v. Washington Public Power

System, the court found that the Contractor failed to give notice of claim pursuant to the contract between the Owner and the General, even though Sime's contract had no notice requirements. It did, however, incorporate by reference the "contract between the owner and the contractor"; thus, failure to give notice barred the claim.

Whether language regarding notice procedure is incorporated by reference or specifically set forth in the contract between parties, notice of a claim must be given pursuant to the procedure outlined in the contract. Washington courts have so held. In Absher Construction Co. v. Kent School District, the contract had a 14 day notice requirement. The court found that this notice requirement could not be waived without an explicit writing. Failure to give the notice or have a waiver in writing was an absolute bar to the claim. When applying the sample language above, a party that fails to give the notice within the 21 days may find their claim barred, no matter the merits of the claim.

In addition to the time requirements for notice, the contract may require the notice to include: (1) the dollar amount of the claim; and (2) a detailed description of the claim itself. This contract language is just as enforceable as the timing requirements. Absher Construction v. Kent School District, is once again an example of such a requirement being enforced. Here, the contract language specified that the notice was to include the amount of the claim and/or the length of delay. The court determined that Absher's use of the language "to be determined" and "cost implication" in its notice was not specific enough to fulfill the contract requirement. Obviously, Absher learned the hard way that notice requirements in a contract must be adhered to and cannot be considered mere "guidelines" for compliance.

Before one concludes that noncompliance with the notice requirements is too harsh, it must be kept in mind that parties to a contract need to receive timely notice and description of any claims in order to determine if alternate means are available to accomplish the work or at least to balance the desirability of any action against possible costs, to mitigate the costs, and not least of all, give parties the opportunity to provide the contractually required notices up the contract chain.

Clearly, all those involved in a construction project who has executed a construction contract must be aware of the notice of claims procedure in their contracts. Administering the contract pursuant to the contract language should ensure that no claim is barred due to a simple oversight in giving the proper notice.

USING THE EICHLEAY FORMULA TO CALCULATE HOME OFFICE OVERHEAD ON CONSTRUCTION DELAY CLAIMS

By: James H. Hopkins, JD SPHR

Construction professionals are aware that they operate in a dispute-prone industry. It is also widely known that construction delays are one of the causes for dispute in the construction process.

In the event of a construction delay, the claimant must seek to resolve a two-pronged problem. First, the claimant must establish entitlement, i.e. why payment is due. Secondly, the claimant must establish the dollar amount of damages caused by the other party. While establishing entitlement is often the easier of the two-prong problem, the damages associated with a contract delay could be the most important.

1. Establishing Right to Payment – The claimant must first establish that the other party was the cause of the delay, and that the contract between the parties entitles the claimant to recovery.

2. Establishing Damages – Once liability has been established, the claimant can address damages. Damages in a

construction claim are made up of actual costs flowing from the actions of the at-fault party, and which were reasonably foreseeable at the time the parties entered into the contract. Examples of actual costs which may be recoverable in a dispute are labor, material, job site indirect costs, finance costs, lost profits and unabsorbed home office overhead.

The Eichleay Formula

The unabsorbed home office overhead calculation is often a confusing and misunderstood aspect of actual costs for many construction professionals. However, by applying a principle commonly known as the "Eichleay Formula", a construction professional can arrive at an appropriate amount, which is likely to be supported by a trier of fact. The Board of Contract Appeals and the Federal Courts now recognize the Eichleay Formula as a means to calculate the amount of unabsorbed home office overhead on federal projects. In addition, the Washington Court of Appeals has approved the Eichleay Formula as a method of calculating damages in Washington.

- Requirements of the Formula

In order to use the Eichleay Formula as a means of calculating unabsorbed home office overhead, two conditions must be met: (1) the claimant was required to stand by during the delay; and (2) the contractor was unable to take on additional work during the time of the delay.

- Implementing the Formula

Implementing the Eichleay Formula is a three-step process. First the claimant must find the allocable overhead by multiplying the total overhead cost incurred during the contract period by the ratio of billings from the delayed contract to the total billings of the contractor during the contract period. Secondly, the claimant must calculate the daily overhead contract rate by dividing the allocable contract overhead by the number of days of contract performance. Finally, the claimant must determine the amount of unabsorbed office overhead by multiplying the number of days of the delay by the daily contract overhead rate.

This process is demonstrated in a mathematical equation below:

<u>Delayed Contract Billings</u>   Total Home Office

$$\frac{\text{Contractor's Total Billings} \times \text{Overhead}}{} = \text{Allocable Home Office Overhead}$$

$$\frac{\text{Allocable Home Office Overhead}}{\text{Days Required to Perform for the Delayed Contract}} = \text{Daily Overhead Rate}$$

Daily Overhead Rate x Number of Days of Delay = Overhead Damages

Although the courts do not require damages to be established with a degree of mathematical certainty, the Eichleay Formula gives the claimant a basis for this calculation.

- Applying the Formula

The application of the Eichleay Formula is the area that causes the most difficulty. Although the use of the formula is recognized as a legitimate method for calculating unabsorbed home office overhead, it does not automatically mean that such damages are recoverable in every delay case. For instance, if the claimant fails to establish that the delay kept the claimant from pursuing other work as required under the Formula, the damages are not recoverable. The claimant must also be ready to face challenges to the overhead items included in calculating the total overhead figure.

In addition, some contracts and the Federal Acquisition Regulations will identify what allowable items and associated costs can be included in the overhead calculations. The claimant must take this into consideration when putting together the components of the Formula.

The time to prepare for a damage claim is at the beginning of any project. By keeping good records and maintaining open communication throughout the project, disputes are likely to be minimized and will go a long way to resolving disputes which do arise. If necessary, the records will also assist in establishing entitlement and the amount of damages.

DAMAGES WHICH FLOW FROM THE BREACH OF A CONSTRUCTION CONTRACT

By: James H. Hopkins, JD SPHR

When a breach of contract occurs, the non-breaching party can recover damages based on two broad categories: (1) direct damages; and (2) consequential damages. The theory for recovery for a breach of a construction contract is no different.

Direct Damages

Direct damages are those arising out of an increase in the cost of the project. Examples of direct damages may include mobilization, demobilization, cost associated with an increase in labor, material or equipment on the project and/or an increase in the overhead associated with the project.

Consequential Damages

Consequential damages are those that are a consequence of the contract breach although not directly flowing from it. These damages could be lost profits, harm to ones business reputation, increased interest expense, and/or lost income.

Calculating Damages

Although the Courts do not require that a specific dollar amount of damages claimed be shown, they do, however, require calculations that are more likely than not to establish the dollars of the claim. The methodology for calculating the dollar amount of claims has been established in basically four forms.

The first (and simplest) is known as the total cost approach. With this approach the damages are calculated by subtracting the bid on the project or the estimated cost of completion from the total actual cost for the completion of the project. The Courts have allowed this methodology; but it does have its weaknesses, specifically, it must assume the reasonableness of the original bid and does not take into consideration the cause of cost

over runs, other than those caused by the party against whom the claim is made. In an attempt to make the total cost approach more acceptable, a four-way test has been developed. The four prongs to this test are: (1) the claimant's actual total costs must be accurate and reasonable; (2) the increased costs must be the result of the breaching party's action (this is the ultimate in the clean hands theory for the claimant); (3) the bid/contract price must be reasonable and prepared properly; and (4) there must not be any other basis upon which the damages can be calculated.

The second method for calculating damages is known as the modified total cost approach. This is the same as the total cost approach, but further refines the damages by deducting any increases in the cost of the project that were the result of the claimant's actions, not so clean hands.

The third methodology is known as the discrete cost approach. Under this method, the claimant identifies all the costs associated with the breach, which then becomes the amount of the claim.

The fourth methodology is called quantum merit approach; meaning, "as much as deserved". This approach is best used when the project has changed so substantially that the original contract and cost estimates are not valid. This method rests on the assumption that the project is basically a different project and the claimant is entitled to recover all reasonable cost associated with completing the project, including profit and overhead costs.

When using the discrete cost approach or quantum meruit approach, the claimant must further identify the cause of the damages as: (1) delay, (2) disruption, (3) changed conditions, (4) change in scope, and/or (5) termination. Delays can be caused by defective drawings, the lack of cooperation from the breaching party, lack of access to the project and/or drawings not being provided in a timely manner. Delay claims are generally based

on those costs related to time rather than volume. Some examples would be equipment rental, worker's pay, or anything that costs more because of a longer time to complete the project. Disruption claims are closely linked to delay costs, in that disruption may cause multiple mobilizations and demobilization or other costs associated with time. Changed conditions occur when the claimant believed the work could be done in one way, but after the work commenced, a condition was discovered that required the work to be performed in a completely different manner. Changed conditions claims are more difficult to price, and for that reason, may be more susceptible to the total cost or modified total cost approach. Change in scope damages occur when the work to been done increases in scope after the contract is executed or after work has commenced. These cost are volume and time driven. Finally, the damages, which would flow from a termination of the contract, would entitle the claimant to profits that would have been earned, but for the wrongful termination.

Conclusion

As in any breach of contract action, a claim in the construction field is a numbers game. These numbers must be accurately maintained throughout the project, rather than created after the dispute arises.

CREDIT TODAY
DOCTOR CREDIT COLUMN

By: James H. Hopkins JD SPHR

The Situation:

A credit professional receives notice that the Chapter 13 Bankruptcy Petition filed by a debtor has been dismissed, and any discharges that may have been entered are revoked.

The Question:

What does this mean to this or any other creditor of the debtor?

Answer:

Any Court may dismiss a bankruptcy petition. The Court will look at the "totality of the circumstances" when making this decision. These are (1) whether the debtor misrepresented facts in the plan or petition; (2) the debtor's history of filings and dismissals; (3) whether the debtor only intended to defeat state court litigation; and (4) whether egregious behavior is present.

In the event of a dismissal, the bankruptcy case is undone to the extent practicable. This means that property is restored to its pre-petition position.

Given the above-referenced facts, the creditor could commence collection action against the debtor, just as if the bankruptcy petition had never been filed.

THE "ECONOMIC LOSS DOCTRINE" IN WASHINGTON

By James H. Hopkins JD SPHR

Every construction professional wants to protect themselves from damages on projects. It would be reasonable to believe that the way to do so is to simply have a clear understanding of the terms and conditions of the construction contract associated with the project. To be sure, this will prevent a multitude of potential problems, but construction professionals must be aware that their protection, even with a contract, is limited by exceptions to the economic loss doctrine. Economic loss has been defined as a loss in value of a product caused by the failure of the product to function as represented, or in other words, a failure of economic expectations. This loss of economic expectation, without any claim of personal injury or damage to other property, may be in the form of lost profit due to delay or increased operating costs.

In Stuart v Coldwell Banker, the Washington Supreme Court also addressed damages by stating: "[w]here only the defective product is damaged, the court should identify whether the particular injury amounts to economic loss or physical damage." This distinction is important because economic losses are not recoverable damages under tort law, and the contract governs liability and recovery for only those in privity of contract.

Initially, the Courts believed that expectancy interests were better resolved without the Court's involvement. In cases where there was only property damage and no contract privity, there was no recovery. The parties were left to allocate risk during contract negotiations. This was considered a "bright-line" rule and was believed to give predictability to the risks associated with construction contracting.

The Washington Supreme Court later reversed its thinking and rejected the opinion that "by restricting product injury claims to contract theories, . . . manufacturers [were given] the means to limit their liabilities to predictable plaintiffs and manageable sums." WPP v Graybar Electric Co. Presumably, the Court decided "the little guy" was not receiving equal protection in this scenario and concluded "… this increased certainty comes at a too high a price".

The State Supreme Court considered the economic loss doctrine in a construction context under the Washington Products Liability Act (WPLA) in WPP v Graybar Electric Co. There, the customer, WWP, attempted to recover damages under the WPLA and in tort from the manufacturer and the distributor for the manufacturer's allegedly faulty insulators. The Court found that the WPLA does not allow recovery under a tort theory of economic loss and left recovery for claims of product injury to contract theories. It did, however, open the door for exceptions to the economic loss doctrine: (1) under a sudden impact and dangerous test and (2) under an evaluative approach. The sudden impact exception will govern when the failures or damages are the result of a sudden and dangerous event. The evaluative approach examines the interrelated factors affecting the failure, such as the nature of the defect, the type of risk, and the manner in which the failure or damages arose. Applying these exceptions, the Washington Courts have allowed recovery of economic loss to the owner of a grain storage building who sued the general contractor and metal fabricator subcontractor after his building collapsed once it had been filled with grain. The Washington Supreme Court held that the damages arose out of a "sudden and dangerous" or "calamitous" event, and the plaintiff was allowed to seek damages in tort for the economic losses. Touchet Balley Grain Growers, Inc. v Opp & Seibold Constr. Inc.

In another case, the Courts rejected economic loss damages involving a contractor attempting to recover for delay damages. The Washington Supreme Court found "[t]here is a beneficial effect to society when contractual agreements are enforced and expectancy interests are not frustrated. In cases involving construction disputes, the conracts entered into among the various parties shall govern their economic expectations. The preservation of the contract represents the most efficient and fair manner in which to limit liability and govern economic expectations in the construction business." Berschauer/Phillips v Seattle School Dist.

The distinction between these two cases is the absence of one of the two exceptions recognized by the Courts when evaluating whether the economic loss doctrine will rule or whether the contract will be the enforcing agent.

What does this mean to anyone who is entering into a construction contract? It means that all parties to a construction contract must be clear about their obligations and expectations. Parties may attempt to negotiate terms and conditions in a contract that will allocate risks and therefore limit their liability. The ability to successfully do so is dependent upon one's bargaining position. Even when successfully allocating the risk, success will only be realized when there is a problem and the party having the risk has the financial where-with-all to absorb that risk.

EMPLOYEE MISCONDUCT AND SAFETY PROGRAMS

By: James H. Hopkins JD SPHR

Job site safety is everyone's responsibility. This is true in theory and practice, especially when Safety Inspectors from the Washington State Department of Labor & Industry (L&I) arrive at a job site to investigate an accident or conduct a job site inspection pursuant to the Washington Industrial Safety and Health Act (WISHA). To even have a possibility of keeping a citation from being issued or defending a citation after it is issued a contractor must have a safety program that is "effective in practice". To accomplish this, the safety program must be in writing and must have been communicated to all employees. When all of that is in place, what happens when an individual employee chooses to work in an unsafe manner, disregarding the employers' safety program? The Washington State Legislature amended WISHA and incorporated what the Courts had previously recognized, "unpreventable employee misconduct" as a basis for no citation being issued by L&I Inspectors. To fall within the confines of this section of WISHA, the following must be in place: 1) a thorough safety program, including work rules, training, and equipment designed to prevent a violation, 2) adequate communication of these rules to employees, 3) steps to be taken to discover and correct violations of the employer's safety rules, and 4) an effective enforcement of the safety program by the employer. The enforcement must be actually practiced and not just a theory.

The purpose behind this section is sound, for employers learned long ago they can not be the insurers of their employees actions. This section sets out, in theory, the limits expected of employers when it comes to job site safety. One-on-one employee-management supervision is not only impractical but is also an affront to skilled workers and crafts.

Most employers raising employee misconduct as a basis for keeping a citation from being issued or defending against an issued citation, can raise sufficient facts to mount the first two rungs of the employee misconduct ladder. Those first two rungs of the employee misconduct ladder being 1) a thorough safety program in place as it relates to the specific activity giving rise to the potential citation and 2) an adequate communication program, specifically, employee training and documentation of the work rules which have been violated.

The best-prepared and most successful contractors with good, implemented safety programs that are effective in practice focus on rungs three and four of the employee misconduct ladder. To accomplish this contractors should routinely document supervisor and/or safety committee safety checks or audits. A completed checklist is an excellent way of establishing the steps taken to discover safety violations, but so can a project supervisor's time-dated notebook with "in compliance," employee counseling, employee warnings, and similar notations of the activities checked for safety.

Documenting worker "compliance" with the day, time and the fact that all safety equipment is being used and /or worn properly, is just as important as documenting and disciplining when a non-compliance situation occurs.

The fourth rung requires the documenting of violations as will as the discipline given for the violation. This is no different than any other area of the employer/employee relationship. Any documentation of employee misconduct should contain the employee's name, state the bases of the offense, the safety regulation violated, the date of the violation and the discipline given, along with any other comments deemed appropriate. Without such documentation, it is difficult to get a foothold on that fourth rung of the employee misconduct ladder, discipline "when violations are discovered."

The basis of an "effective" safety program, which is the criteria a WISHA Inspector will utilize when determining whether a citation should be issued, is how well is the safety program is working. Basically do the employees' understand and acknowledge, they knew they could be disciplined for not complying with the safety program; were diligent safety audits or checks conducted and did prompt, appropriate discipline occur.

WISHA inspectors will also judge a safety programs' effectiveness by the number and type of citations a contractor has received in the past. That is yet another reason why employers should make careful decisions in evaluating their options for dealing with safety violations at a job site. The area of safety violations needs to take the same priority in the employer/employee relationship as drugs at the jobsite, absenteeism and any other violation of the work rules. Without this employees can be injured and employers cited for WISHA violations which could be avoided.

THE EMPLOYER/EMPLOYEE RELATIONSHIP BEGINS BEFORE THE BEGINNING

By: James H. Hopkins JD SPHR

The employer/employee relationship clearly exists when an employer hires an individual to accomplish a task.

Every employer is aware of his or her responsibilities as it relates to this relationship with regards to safety, nondiscrimination, overtime pay and the like.

But an employer's responsibility to his or her employees begins before the first employee is placed on the payroll. One of the prehire requirements placed on employers is the posting of certain posters in a conspicuous place where all employees can read them. Federal regulations and State regulations identify these posters. The federal posters are outlined below, with the Agency responsible for the regulation. The responsible agency is where an employer would go to obtain a copy of the appropriate poster.

Name of Poster	Posting Requirements Agency Responsible
Minimum Wage	Required for all employers U.S. Dept of Labor, Wage and Hour Division
It's the Law OSHA (English and Spanish)	Required for all employers U.S. Occupational Safety Notice and Health Administration
Notice to Workers With Disabilities (English and Spanish)	Required for all employers U.S. Equal Employment Opportunity Commission
Employee Polygraph (English and Spanich)	Required for all employers U.S. Dept of Labor, Employment Protection Standards of workers
Employee Polygraph (English and Spanish)	Required for all employers U.S. Dept of Labor, Wage and Hour Protection Division
Family and Medical Leave Act	Required for all employers of 50 or more employees U.S. Dept of Labor, Wage and Hour Division

Migrant & Seasonal   Required for all employers
U.S. Dept of Labor, Wage and Hour
Division Protection of migrant workers
Agriculture Worker
(English and Spanish)

Check Your Withholding Recommended for all
employers
Internal Revenue Service

Earned Income Credit Recommended for all
employers
Internal Revenue Service

As can be seen these posters are as varied in their topics as the agencies that administer the various requirements.

Employment Applications

When it becomes necessary for an employer to hire a new employee, each applicant should be required to complete an employment application. Doing so will serve several purposes: (1) establish a record of who applies for position; (2) serve as a source of prospects for future hiring; and (3) assist in determining qualified candidates.

An employment application can take many forms. One over another is not necessarily good or bad. The main point is to ensure that the application does not seek discriminatory information regarding health, age, race, sex, etc; but, rather, but does seek the qualifications that the applicant has which will make him or her successful in the position for which they are applying. It is recommended that every applicant be required to complete and sign an employment application. In the event the employer only receives a resume from a prospective applicant, it is recommended that the applicant be required to sign and date the resume. Generally, when someone signs information, they understand that the accuracy of that information is important. In addition, any disciplinary action will be easier to defend, should it be discovered subsequent to hiring an individual, that she/he has been less than truthful on their resume and/or application.

The employer will use the application and an applicant interview to help reach a hiring decision. The employer will seek information which establishes the applicant's ability to perform the job, as identified in the position description. This needs to be done by seeking information that establishes the applicant's experience, education and skills. Information regarding age (other than if the applicant is over the age of 18), religion, national origin or other unlawful information must not be sought.[1] English only rules are also suspect.[2] English only rules in the workplace are permissible only when required by a business necessity.3

GENERAL SUMMARY

ESSENTIAL FUNCTIONS

SCOPE OF RESPONSIBILITY

SPECIFIC SKILLS REQUIRED

EDUCATION AND EXPERIENCE REQUIRED

GENERAL WORKING CONDITIONS

The categories contained in this job description are not necessarily all-inclusive; additional duties may be assigned and requirements may vary from time to time.

The one thing every employer should keep in mind anytime an investigator comes to an employer's premise is one of the first things they ask is to see where these posters are posted. Getting off on the right foot with an investigator is a good thing. Having the appropriate poster posted is a small price to pay.

---

1   This could also apply to height and weight inquiries; 29 C.F.R. §1606.6.

2   29 C.F.R. § 1606.7.
3   Long v. First Union Corp. of Va., 894 F. Supp. 933 (E.D. Va. 1995).

THE FAIR LABOR STANDARDS ACT (FLSA)

Ellen C. Kearns, editor-in-chief
BNA Publications
1999; 2001 Cumulative Supplement

Is It More Than an 1,800-page Doorstop? A Resounding "Yes!"

By: James H. Hopkins JD SPHR

Ellen C. Kearns's treatise on the Fair Labor Standards Act (FLSA) is to wage-and-hour law as Grossman is to discrimination law. Ms. Kearns is supported in her effort by a prominent group of contributing editors, including WSBA members Thomas W. McLane, who contributed to "Hot Goods Violations"; and Timothy J. Pauley, who contributed to "Record Keeping." I heartily recommend this volume to firms that enforce, defend or prosecute FSLA and its attendant regulations established by the Wage and Hour Division of the U.S. Department of Labor.

Originally published in 1999, this book includes a 2001 cumulative supplement, current through the latter part of 2000, published under the guidance of Editor-in-Chief Monica Gallagher. Although the material contained in this volume may be obtained through different sources, it is notable that the editors have compiled the information under one roof, saving readers much effort.

When this work was commissioned, the Labor and Employment section of the American Bar Association stated its goals in the foreword of the cumulative supplement: "(1) to be equally balanced and nonpartisan in their viewpoints"; and (2) "to ensure the book is of significant value to the practitioner, student, and sophisticated non-lawyer." I believe these goals have been realized.

The book begins with a historical perspective, moves into a general overview, and ends with specific discussions of the various portions of the FLSA. A general plus of the volume is that the editors have cited cases from a variety of circuits, giving perspective to practitioners in various areas around the country. Since the FLSA does not pre-empt the field, various state statutes and case law are relevant to the practitioner. While using this book, attorneys must be cognizant of this, and should apply its information in coordination with these statutes. The editors have done a good job of keeping the reader apprised of this situation.

Great detail is given to the nuances of the act, and areas the daily practitioner may not often encounter. One example is the exemption established for home workers who make wreaths, as long as the wreath is made up of "natural holly, pine, cedar or other evergreens." If the editors have found this obscure exemption, we may feel safe that they have included those that practitioners use on a regular basis.

I have often struggled with determining the "regular rate" of pay to use for calculating overtime compensation. In its "Determining Overtime Compensation" chapter, this book does a good job of explaining the fine distinctions of this knotty problem. In addition, examples explain the administration of the different calculations.

Child labor is a topic that is very much in the news today, especially as it applies to industries that move operations to other countries, thereby placing themselves in the position of using child labor. As the 21st century begins, it has been less than a 100 years since the Triangle Shirtwaist Factory fire in New York City, where 146 women and children between the ages of 13 and 23 died. It is difficult to believe that the FLSA, the definitive answer to child labor in the United States, was not passed by Congress until 1937 — 26 years after this tragedy. Nor did the U.S. Supreme Court overrule its previous decision overturning a child-labor statute until 1941. With this in mind, are other countries' attitudes regarding child labor that far behind the United States? The editors provide a historical perspective of the various sections of the statute, lending an understanding of the "why," to help practitioners administer the "what" more effectively.

The editors are so thorough they have even included a short chapter aptly called "Homework." Before parents become too concerned, let me explain that this refers to a ban on work performed at home in an attempt by companies to go around the FLSA. I must admit I have never had to refer to this section in 30 years of working in this area; but once again it is an example of the attention to detail paid by the editors and could become more of an issue in this era of cyberspace.

The volume contains a solid briefing on the record-keeping requirements of the FLSA. When complied with, this is one area of the FLSA that will keep employers out of trouble. This assumes, of course, that the records reflect the employer's compliance with the act. Although the editors have stated: "[T]he regulations do not establish any single acceptable system of record-keeping," I would have liked to have seen a sample for maintaining records of hours worked, straight-time hours, and overtime hours in the appendix. The chapter on "Record-Keeping" provides enough detail on the types of records to keep and the duration for retention that anyone should be able to develop an adequate record-keeping system.

The chapters "Enforcement and Remedies" and "Litigation Issues" comprise approximately a quarter of the volume, and offer insight into remedies ranging from administrative review to criminal sanctions. As an example, in a situation where an employee has a calendar reflecting times worked and the employer has kept no record, the administrative agency or hearing court must rely on only one set of documents, and the burden is on the employer to prove that the employee's documentation is inaccurate. A situation such as this clearly illustrates the importance of the record-keeping chapter, and may prevent the employer from a required review of the "Remedies" and "Litigation" chapters. These latter chapters are as detailed and helpful as all the previous ones discussed.

I give The Fair Labor Standards Act, published by BNA, an enthusiastic two thumbs up.

INDIVIDUAL LIABILTY FOR CORPORATE ACTS BY BOARD OF DIRECTORS POST ENRON/WORLDCOM

By: James H. Hopkins, JD SPHR

Following the disclosure of questionable, and/or illegal actions at Enron, WorldCom, Arthur Andersen, etc., the need for all members of a Corporation's Board of Directors to understand and appreciate their personal exposure for decisions made in their official capacity is heightened.

As we have seen recently, exuberant spending of corporate funds for personal aggrandizement may go unchallenged when the Stakeholders (i.e. Shareholders, other members of the Board of Directors, Officers, Employees, government oversight agencies, vendors, and customers), and others are benefiting financially. However, tough economic times will lead to more frequent challenges to Directors' actions, as current events have demonstrated. With the heavy media attention now being given to the actions of even the most respected corporations, Stakeholders and other interested parties are much better informed and far more apt to question corporate decisions and practices by the Corporation's Board of Directors.

Board of Directors' Standard of Care

Above all else, the members of the Board of Directors of a corporation are required to "act in good faith, with the care an ordinary prudent person would exercise under similar circumstances in a manner situated and in the best interest of the Corporation" according to the Washington State statutes governing corporations doing business in Washington. Courts act on a case-by-case basis when deciding whether Directors have fulfilled their standard of care.

Duties of the Board of Directors

Commentators have defined this standard of care by enumerating various duties: 1) a duty of care; 2) a duty to become informed; 3) a duty of inquiry; 4) a duty of informed judgment; 5) a duty of loyalty; 6) a duty of fair dealing; and 7) a duty of fiduciary responsibility. These duties are not to be compartmentalized, but do in fact overlap.

Functions of the Board of Directors

The Board of Directors basically has two functions:

(1) Decision-Making.

Within this function, the Directors would be called upon to use the duties of care, inquiry, becoming informed, attention, and informed judgment.

(2) Provide Oversight of the Officers of the Corporation.

To perform this function, Directors must utilize the duties of attention, becoming informed and inquiry.

The Directors must ensure they have the information necessary to fulfill these duties, and verify that the information is appropriate and accurate.

Business Judgment Rule

In Washington, the business judgment rule embodies these duties. Directors are insulated by the business judgment rule to the extent they carry out these duties in "good faith" and without "corrupt intent."

To act in good faith is to take reasonable steps to fulfill the duties previously described. This reasonableness must be fulfilled in both the subjective and objective sense.

In the subjective sense, the particular Director must believe the action taken was appropriate.

In the objective sense, the Court will look to whether a similarly situated Director would have thought the action taken was appropriate. The reasonable believe that the action taken was appropriate is best described as, did the Director taking the action possess common sense, a practical wisdom and make an informed judgment, and fulfill her/his duties.

In addition to the good faith element of the business judgment rule, there is a second element wherein the action taken must be in the best interest of the Corporation.

The Directors have wide discretion in determining the best interest of the Corporation when weighing opportunities versus benefits and how the various Stakeholders in the Corporation may benefit or suffer. Clearly, a benefit to one group could be a detriment to another (i.e. paying bonuses to Employees versus paying a dividend to Shareholders)

.

An individual Board Member's personal liability may come from any of the other Stakeholders of the corporation.

The members of the Board of Directors will find themselves in different situations that could expose them to this liability.

Conflicts and Interest

In the event any Director has a conflict of interest in any decision; a breach of their good faith requirement may be apparent. A conflict of interest is when the individual Director or any person related to the Director or any entity the Director has an interest in has an interest in the outcome of the decision being made by the Board of Directors.

Corporation's Indemnity and Defense

In the past, an often times unwritten standard existed in the corporate climate to indemnify and defend individual Directors against inquiries or actions taken against the individual Director for corporate decisions he or she may have made. This code of corporate behavior may have lulled Directors into a false sense of security. In the present economic environment, a corporations is more likely than ever to be facing economic difficulties and therefore have fewer resources to defend individual Directors. The other members of the Board of Directors may deem it not in the corporation's best interest to defend an individual Director. Finally the party claiming to be wronged may only be able to recover damages from the individual. Relying on the deep pockets of the corporation to indemnify and defend an individual Director's action is not a good plan. The only strategy that should come into play is competence and compliance.

Conclusion

All decisions made by Directors should be based on the underlying assumption of how the action will benefit the Corporation (the entity) not the individual (Director).

MECHANIC'S AND MATERIALMAN'S LIENS -- STRICT COMPLIANCE WITH STATUTE REQUIRED

By: James H. Hopkins JD SPHR

As the members of NACM know, the Mechanic's and Materialman's Lien Statute provides additional security beyond sound credit practices for those businesses that work on or provide materials for construction projects.

This protection is a creation of the Washington State Legislature and can be found at RCW 60.04 et al. Because it is legislated, it can be modified by the state legislature. Therefore, NACM's Legislative Task Force continually monitors the legislature actions in this regard.

The Courts have consistently held that because the lien statute is a creation of the legislature, claimants must strictly comply with its requirements. The Washington Court of Appeals has once again reiterated that policy in a recent case. The statute states that the claim of lien "[s]hall be signed by the claimant or some person authorized to act on his or her behalf who shall affirmatively state they have read the notice of claim of lien and believe the notice of claim of lien to be true and correct under penalty of perjury, and shall be acknowledged."

The signature requirements in the form provided with the NACM Lien Manual are taken directly from the statute and provide places for signatures (see below).

A_____, Claimant
_____
(Phone number, address, city and state of claimant)

STATE OF WASHINGTON)
) SS.
COUNTY OF   )

                                                                ,
being sworn, says: I am the claimant (or attorney of the claimant, or administrator, representative, or agent of the trustees of an employee benefit plan) above-named; I have read or heard the foregoing claim, read and know the contents thereof, and believe the same to be true and correct and that the claim of lien is not frivolous and is made with reasonable cause, and is not clearly excessive under penalty of perjury.

By:_____

I certify that I know or have satisfactory evidence that

is the person who appeared before me, and said person acknowledged that _____ signed this instrument and acknowledged it to be _____ free and voluntary act for the uses and purposes mentioned in the instrument.

Dated: .

NOTARY PUBLIC in and for the State of Washington, residing at
My Commission expires:

In the recent case, the claimant had signed on line A, but not on line B. The Court concluded that this was not in compliance with the statute, and the lien was dismissed.

The moral of this story is clear: when credit professionals are using the Mechanic's and Materialman's Statute as part of their credit package, strict compliance must be the rule; close does not count.

LIMITATIONS OF LIABILITY CLAUSES: IGNORANCE IS NOT BLISS

By: James H. Hopkins, JD SPHR*

Contract clauses purporting to limit the amount of damages for which a party to a contract may be liable have been a part of the contracting process for a number of years in Washington. In fact, the Washington Supreme Court recognized such a clause as early as 1967 in Fleming v Stoddard Wendle Motor Co. There, the Court said it would recognize limitation of liability clauses when such provisions "clearly express an intention to exclude liability." In the construction context, such a clause may take several forms: limiting the liability of a party to a liquidated amount or only an extension of time for delays; compensatory damages but not consequential damages; or an indemnity or hold harmless provision. Such clauses are part of the standard AIA Document A201 commonly used in the construction industry. No matter the form such clauses take, they are part of the negotiating process and reflect the bargain for intent of the parties to the contract.

In a recent Washington State Supreme Court decision, a local general contractor discovered that Washington courts would enforce such limitations of liability clauses, whether or not the terms are "presented in a contractual, meaningful way."

The situation arose when the general contractor used a software developer's computer program to prepare its bid for a large construction project. The general contractor's euphoria in being the low bidder was short-lived when it discovered that the software utilized in preparing the bid apparently had under-calculated the bid by approximately two million dollars.

The general contractor purchased the software from a software company and had assistance with installation from a third party. The purchase was made with the general contractor's purchase order form. The software was shipped and delivered in shrink-wrap packages. The manufacturer's licensing agreement was in the shrink-wrap packaging, along with the diskettes and instruction manual. It is unclear whether the general contractor or the third party installer opened the shrink-wrap; however, to the Court this didn't seem to matter.

The terms of the licensing agreement provided that if the purchaser did not want to be bound by the terms and conditions of the license agreement, they could return the software. During the installation process or during the bid preparation process, the software generated numerous error messages. At some point it was discovered that the software developer was aware of the error messages, but did not believe that they would cause a major problem.

After discovering the flaw in the product, the general contractor brought a lawsuit against the software developer for the damages caused when the software generated the low bid.

The software developer defended the lawsuit based upon the limitations of liability clause in the license agreement, which was contained in the shrink wrap packaging. The pertinent part of the license agreement stated: "[the software developer's] liability for damages in no event shall exceed the license fee paid for the right to use the programs." The Court held that pursuant to the Uniform Commercial Code, the terms of the licensing agreement, and the general contractor's use of the software, the limitations of liability language above were a part of the contract. It therefore became part of the general contractor's agreement with the software developer. This has become common in all software that is being shipped today. The Court went so far as to state: "[i]t was not necessary for [the general contractor] to actually read the agreement in order to be bound by it."

Based on the Court's findings, it concluded that the software developer was not liable for the damages caused by its product having been responsible for the general contractor's underbid. However, in quoting the trial judge, the Court stated that "if this case had arisen in 1985 rather than 1997" the ruling may have been different. The Court's statement was probably of little solace to the general contractor who had the misfortune of being on the wrong end of the Court's timeline.

In certain arenas of construction law, the enforceability of limitation of liability clauses may not be well settled in Washington, but clearly with regard to software licensing, the question seems to have been answered conclusively.

Because most, if not all, businesses rely increasingly upon data generated with the use of software-driven computers, the risk of losses in the thousands or millions (as with this general contractor) are not uncommon when a faulty software product is installed. In such an event, the recovery allowed by the limitation of liability for the cost of the software is often no more than an insult after injury.

If the general contractor in this example were able to provide advice to others in the industry, it would no doubt stress a greater importance on the review of the limitation of liability clause prior to the use of the product, especially when dealing with software. This preventive measure should be an easy step for businesses to take to protect themselves from being in this unlucky general contractor's shoes.

* Mr. Hopkins represents business clients in all areas of matters relating to business and commercial transactions, as well as situations relating to the employer/employee relationship. Mr. Hopkins has 20 years' experience assisting business in these areas.

MANAGING EMPLOYEE ABSENTISM IN WASHINGTON

By James H. Hopkins, JD SPHR

When an employee works a standard five-day week, one can assume 260 workdays exist annually. After subtracting ten days on average for vacation and another ten days for federal, state and local holidays, an employer could expect 240 work days a year per employee.

Traditional Methods Of Managing Absenteeism

Managing absenteeism for these 240 days has historically been straightforward. Work-related injuries were handled pursuant to the State Worker's Compensation Laws. In Washington, any employer with one or more employees must comply with these State Worker's Compensation Laws.

Other absences were handled under the employer's policies relating to absences or pursuant to a Collective Bargaining Agreement (CBA). A company's absence policy would inform employees in advance of the employer's attendance expectations. Most CBA would contain provisions relating to attendance expectations. A typical policy or CBAs would provide for a progressive discipline procedure for unexcused absences. Thus, one such absence would warrant a warning and subsequent absences might lead to termination.

Additional Laws Governing Absenteeism

Today employers must not only comply with company policies and/or a CBA and Worker's Compensation Laws, but also The Americans with Disabilities Act (ADA) if it employs fifteen or more employees for twenty weeks in any given year. In addition, The Family Medical Leave Act (FMLA) is applicable to employers with fifty or more employees, if the employees work within a seventy-five-mile radius of the employer's premises for at least twenty weeks in any given year.

Which law applies?

Generally, the ADA only applies to permanent or long-term conditions. Although there could be a work-related injury that causes a permanent disability under Worker's Compensation, injuries governed by Worker's Compensation are predominately temporary with no long-term impact. By the same token, it is possible that a work-related injury will fall within the confines of the ADA, and this must be evaluated. Most work-related injuries would not fall within the purview of The FMLA.

Whether the ADA and the FMLA will cover the same injury is unlikely, as the definition of a disability under the ADA is more restrictive than under the FMLA.
Whereas the FMLA requires the granting of time-off for an employee for a non-employee illness or injury, the ADA and the Worker's Compensation laws are restricted to illness or injury to the employee.

In the event an employer is subject to the FMLA, ADA and/or Worker's Compensation laws, absences which fall under these laws cannot be considered when taking disciplinary action under a company policy or CBA.

Requirements for Coverage

After determining that it is subject to one or more of these laws, the employer must consider whether a particular situation meets the requirements for coverage under the applicable law or laws.

FMLA: Employees are eligible for leave under the FMLA if they meet certain requirements: (1) the individual has been employed by the employer for at least twelve months (it is not required that the twelve months be consecutive); and (2) the employee has worked at least 1,250 hours in the past twelve months.

ADA: The ADA protects employees who have a qualifying disability. The employee must be: (1) considered disabled pursuant to the law; (2) qualified to do the work; and (3) able to perform the essential functions of the job with a reasonable accommodation. A reasonable accommodation is generally defined as an alteration to the work environment in order for the disabled individual to (a) perform the essential functions of the job; (b) enjoy equal benefits and privileges of employment; and (c) be considered for an available position. A reasonable accommodation is not required if it will cause an undue hardship on the employer. To determine if an undue hardship will be caused, an employer must consider: (1) the nature and cost of the accommodation; (2) the overall financial resources of the employer; (3) the size, organization and function of the employers' workforce; (4) the number of facilities operated by the employer; and (5) the intrusiveness of the accommodation.

Worker's Compensation: To be eligible for Worker's Compensation the employee's injuries must job related.

Compliance in Calculating Leave

Once an employer has established that the laws apply to a qualified event, the next step in compliance is to determine how much leave an employee is entitled to receive, if any.

FMLA: The FMLA allows an employee, male or female, to take up to twelve weeks leave per year for one or more of the following reasons: (1) birth of a baby or the care for a newborn; (2) care of an adopted child or foster child; (3) care for the employee's spouse, child or parent with a serious health condition; and (4) because of a serious health condition that renders the employee unable to perform his/her job. A serious health condition under the FMLA is defined as an illness or injury that involves (a) a period of hospital treatment; (b) a period of incapacity requiring absence from work; (c) an incapacity due to pregnancy or prenatal care; or (d) a period of absences for treatment of a chronic medical condition. Under FMLA the year of leave can be calculated using: (e) the calendar year; (f) any fixed twelve month period; (g) the twelve month period measured forward from when the FMLA time off began; or (h) a rolling twelve-month period measured backwards from when the FMLA time off began. The employer can pick the time measurement wanted, but, once established, it must be consistent.

ADA: Under the ADA there is no specific time period for time off. The time off falls within the reasonable accommodation requirements discussed earlier.

Worker's Compensation: Under Worker's Compensation, the amount of time off will be dictated by the medical requirements of the injury and the employee's attending physician, although the employer can request an independent medical exam to test the reasonableness of the attending physician's directive.

Conclusion

The first step for the conscientious employer who wants to get work done, be fair to employees and comply with applicable employment laws, is to pay as close attention to their employees and their situation as the employer does to marketing and the collection of accounts receivable. Most employers do not seem to care for this side of the business, and for that reason, appear to shy away from dealing with employer/employee relationship issues. However, when a situation arises and one of the employment laws is violated, it can add a heavy burden to a business' bottom line. Maintaining a clear policy on how absenteeism will be handled when it arises will give employees comfort in knowing the company's expectations in advance and assist managers in being consistent when dealing with employees and complying with employment laws.

MEDICAL PROFESSION UNIONIZED RULES IN A NONUNION ENVIRONMENT

BY James H. Hopkins JD SPHR*

The medical community is familiar with hassles involving insurance companies and Medicaid and Medicare reimbursements, but recently, the National Labor Relations Board (NLRB) and the Courts have been added to the list of worries for the medical profession. Increasingly, the NLRB and the Courts are pursuing violations of the National Labor Relations Act (NLRA) by nonunion employers in traditional nonunion industries, such as the medical profession.

Practices, which were routine for employers to take in the past, are now considered an NLRA violation. Chief among them is having a policy that prohibits employees from discussing their wages and benefits with one another. The Courts have concluded that such prohibition is an unlawful interference with the employees' rights under the NLRA to participate in organizational and concerted activity.

In addition, the NLRB recently ruled that an employee in a nonunion shop must be allowed to have a fellow employee present during a disciplinary conference with management.

Furthermore, an employer may be found to violate the NLRA when they have meetings with groups of employees in an attempt to improve the workplace. In such meetings, the Courts have stated that management can only give out information -- not enter into a dialogue with the employees regarding wages, hours, or working conditions -- for this could be a company dominated union.

Does all this mean the Medical Profession and other employers in the 21st century must operate under a constant threat from the courts and government agencies when they take any steps in dealing with their employees? In short, yes; a real threat always exists. The NLRA should be considered as seriously in a nonunion environment as the wage and hour or discrimination laws. However, employers can take steps to minimize problems and ensure the success of their actions concerning the employer/employee relationship, if challenged either in a court or before a governmental agency.

Some steps that a concerned employer can and should take are:

(1) Have an employee handbook that clearly outlines expectation of employees;

(2) Consistently follow the procedures outlined in the employee handbook;

(3) Ensure that any group meetings are used to gather information or communicate information and/or policy;

(4) Do not have any policy that purports to prohibit employees from discussing their wages hours or working conditions, (this is for two reasons:

    (i) it is a violation of the NLRA, but even more compelling;
    (ii) it will not be followed;

(5) Implement a policy to allow an employee to have a fellow employee sit in on any disciplinary meeting, if requested.

In the final analysis, the best way to minimize the risk of legal problems with employees is not to "Kill all the lawyers" as Shakespeare stated, but to simply treat employees as you would want to be treated. This of course assumes that you wish to be treated fairly, with dignity and respect.

*Mr. Hopkins is an attorney who represents Employers in all phases of the employer/employee relationship in union and nonunion environments.

MILITARY VETERAN'S REEMPLOYMENT RIGHTS

James H. Hopkins JD SPHR

The United States has approximately a half million men and women in the uniforms of the various branches of the military, Army, Navy, Marines Air Force and Coast Guard, all of this because of the military action in the Middle East and the war against terrorism which has been ongoing since September 11, 2001. Of that half million, it is estimated that 30-40 % are reservists called onto active duty with some being first time enlistees.

This means many employers have had or will have employees go onto active duty with the various branches of service. Each employer needs to be aware there are special laws, which give the returning service people certain rights with regard to their reemployment.

The Uniformed Services employment and Reemployment rights Act (USERRA) allows an individual to be absent from work for military duty up to five years. There are some notable exceptions to this rule, for periodic training, involuntary active duty, extensions and recalls during National Emergencies. These exceptions could extend the five-year period. Also up to two additional years will be given in the event the veteran was injured on active duty and the employer must make reasonable efforts to accommodate the disabled returning veteran. The returning veteran has certain responsibilities; they must reapply for their position with their previous employer within certain time restraints. When the active duty period was 1 to 30 days, they must reapply by the first regularly scheduled workday following eight hours after the person returns home, as an example a returning veteran could not be required to report for work at 12:30 p.m. when he/she had returned at 10:00 p.m. but could be required to report for a 7:00 a.m. shift with the same 10:00 p.m. return home time. When the active duty period was 31 days to 180 days the veteran must reapply no later than 14 days after completion being discharged from active duty. When the active duty period is 181 days or longer the veteran must reapply no later than 90 days after completion of his/her active service.

Returning veterans are to be reemployed into positions they would have attained had they not been absent for military service, with the same seniority, status and pay. All of this with the corresponding privileges and benefits that would accrue to them with such seniority. The veteran needs to be awarded any promotion he/she would have received and all, across the board pay raises that would have been granted had they not been on active duty with the military. This clearly means any adjustments in wages for the position they returned to, but could also mean any merit increases they would have received, this will be especially true if merit increases are awarded to nearly all the other employees. Vacation time will not accrue for the time the veteran is on active duty but the time away will be counted towards the seniority for calculating future vacation. This is true of course unless the employer allows individuals on other kinds of leaves, i.e. Family Medical Leave and the like, to accrue vacation while away then of course the veteran must be provided the same privilege. With regard to pension benefits the veteran must be treated as if they had been continuously employed, this means the time on active duty is the same as time worked when the veteran's length of service is considered under a Pension Plan.

The veterans leaving an employer to enter into active military service are also entitled to COBRA benefits along with the privileges and duties thereunder, while on active duty.

The thing all employers must remember is that an employee is entitled to the same treatment while away and upon return as if they had never left.

NEGOTIATIONS AND THE HUMAN RESOURCE PROFESSIONAL

By: James H. Hopkins, JD SPHR

Human Resource professionals continually find themselves in a variety of situations requiring negotiating skills. These situations may range from dealing with managers within one's own organization regarding what policies should be, to employees regarding what policies are, and/or labor unions in collective bargaining.

The Constants in Negotiating

The negotiation process will generally follow a predictable pattern, regardless of who is taking part in the process. The steps, which will make up the process are: (1) preparation; (2) initial meeting; (3) recess; and (4) follow up meeting(s).

A. Preparation

Thorough preparation is the key to any successful negotiations. Until all parties have invested the time and effort in fully preparing themselves, face-to-face negotiations are not practical.

The first step in preparing for negotiations is to conduct objective fact-finding to determine the who, what, when and why of the negotiations.

Who: Those individuals on both sides of the negotiations who will be critical to reaching an agreement. While the personalities of the participants should not play a part, in reality, it is difficult to remove this aspect from the process. Therefore, it may be necessary to incorporate the participants' personalities into the fact-finding mission.

What: Any negotiator must have a clear understanding of the subject matter of the negotiations. The strengths and weaknesses of your team and the other team need to be identified. For example, a Human Resource professional must be aware of the other parties' reasons for taking the position they have, the strengths or weaknesses of their and the other parties' position, and the way any given situation has been handled in the past within the company and/or the company's overall industry.

When: The time frame in which the negotiations must commence and/or be completed need to be identified. If no firm time frame applies, it is still a good idea to establish a time line to keep the process on track and moving forward at a reasonable pace.

Why: Both the desired results and the justification of the results should be known and clearly identified. The ultimate purpose of the negotiations should not be to crush that so-and-so, but to accomplish an economic result.

By answering these questions, one determines the goals for the negotiations in a rational, logical manner.

While establishing your team's goals, the minimal acceptable position and a maximum expected position should be set. The other party to the negotiations will be contemplating this as well. Where these positions overlap will determine the settlement range

B. The Initial Negotiation Meeting

When the preparation process is complete, it is time to commence the actual negotiations. During the initial meeting, the negotiators will put their position on the table, make a general statement as to why they believe their position is just, and verify the information developed during the preparation phase. The amount of information provided to the other side at this time will depend upon many factors -- such as the number of anticipated "follow up" meetings that will take place, the relationship between the negotiators and the overall feeling of the negotiators on how the meeting is going.
At this point, it is important that the parties establish a civil working environment, check egos at the door, and come in with the understanding that the best end result may not make everyone happy, but is one that will be fair to all involved. If a negotiator appears

completely inflexible during this "first date", it may signal the collapse of the negotiations and ensure that there will not be a "second date".

If future meetings are to be held, the negotiators should determine where and when these will happen. It is not uncommon for each side to try hold the meeting(s) in a location designed to give them a "home court" advantage. This advantage may mean meeting at the office of one of the negotiators. To eliminate a possible home court advantage for either party, there may be a benefit to holding the negotiations at a neutral site. The major factor in determining whether this is feasible is the costs associated with a neutral location, and whether the parties are willing to come to an agreement about the division of such costs. Care must be taken not to let this become a core issue of negotiations. Some may recall the Paris Peace Talks in the 1970s where the American and Vietnamese negotiators spent days attempting to resolve conflicts over the shape of the negotiating table. Don't let this happen to you! Preparedness will go a long way toward neutralizing any home court advantage either side may have.

By listening carefully and with thorough preparation, a negotiator will identify early those items the other side appears to deem important and which the negotiator feels are less important to her/his position. This will allow the negotiator to make concessions, which will communicate flexibility to the other side, without core issues being affected; thereby building goodwill. Establishing this relationship early by conceding non-issues may prove to be vital later in the negotiations. The other team may be more willing to concede your major points if they feel you have been more than fair.

C. Recess

The parties should recess after this initial meeting and evaluate the information received as well as their respective position. Such a recess may range from a few minutes to a few days. The time frame set out in the preparation phase may dictate the length of any recess. Another factor in determining the time spent in recess is how long it will take for both sides to digest the information provided and to incorporate this information with the information from the preparation phase.

During this time, the settlement range may be narrowed based upon the give and take explored during the initial meeting.

C. Follow Up Meetings

Depending upon one's strengths and/or weakness an overall bargaining strategy and bargaining style will begin to emerge. This strategy and style will set the tone for any future meetings.

The strategy may be to settle early for less dollars or negotiate --taking a tougher position in an attempt to move higher in the settlement range. Again, keep in mind the goals first established and continue working on separating the people from the issues.

Negotiating styles will depend upon the relationship a negotiator has established with the other side. The style may be affected by prior negotiations between the parties, and/or whether the parties' relationship will continue beyond a particular negotiation or whether this is a one-time transaction.

In the event of a one-time transaction, the style may be firmer, with the negotiator continuing to push the initiative and make little or no concessions. On the other hand, if the relationship must continue beyond these negotiations, a more collaborative approach is sensible.

Conclusion

A good negotiator will focus on being positive during the negotiations, being a good listener, and at all times being considerate of the individuals with whom she/he is negotiating.

Use of objective criteria during negotiation and keeping options open to create mutual gain will generally lead to a satisfactory result.

Mr. Hopkins is member of SHRM's Employee and Labor Relations Committee.

THE PENALTIES EMPLOYERS FACE FOR VIOLATING THE NATIONAL LABOR RELATIONS ACT (NLRA)

By: James H. Hopkins, JD, SPHR

Employers found by the National Labor Relations Board (NLRB) to have violated the NLRA can expect to have a variety of penalties imposed upon them.

The areas of the NLRA that lead to unfair labor practices charges against employers are:

1. Section 8 (a)(1): restricts an employer from interfering with, coercing, or restraining any employee in her or his right to organize a union or bargain collectively with their employer. When an employer has been found to have committed an unfair labor practice in violation of an employee's rights in this area, the NLRB will issue a cease and desist order. The NLRB will also require a notice to be posted for sixty consecutive days at the employer's premises. In situations where an employer has been found to have interfered with the election process to the point that the NLRB does not believe a fair election can be held, it may issue a bargaining order. By issuing such an order, the NLRB will

direct the employer to negotiate with the union without any further election being conducted.

2. Section 8 (a)(2): prohibits an employer from dominating or controlling a union. The NLRB will order such a union disestablished when it finds an employer in violation of this section. The NLRB may also require the employer to repay union dues withheld from the employee's pay per a union security clause negotiated with the employer-dominated union. Where there may have been assistance that does not reach dominating or controlling status, recognition may be ordered withheld until the NLRB certifies the union as reflecting the wishes of the employees.

3. Section 8 (a)(3): restrict an employer from discriminating in the hiring or tenure of an employee because of union membership or the lack thereof. When an employer is found to have violated this section, the NLRB will issue a cease and desist order and require the posting of a notice of the violation. In addition, compensation to the employee who was discriminated against may be ordered, when warranted. Such relief can go beyond just pay to any form of compensation the individual would have received but for the discrimination. When an employer closes an operation rather than deal with a union, the NLRB historically has ordered

the employer to resume operations as an appropriate remedy.

4. Section 8 (a)(4): prohibits the termination of an employee based on his or her union activity. If the NLRB finds a violation of this section, it will issue a cease and desist order, and/or order reinstatement of and back pay for the employee. Just as under Section 8 (a)(3), this form of relief can go beyond pay to any form of compensation the individual would have received, but for the termination due to the union activity.

5. Section 8 (a)(5): requires employers to bargain in good faith with the employee's chosen union representative. In the event the NLRB determines that a failure to bargain in good faith exists, it will issue a cease and desist order and an affirmative order directing the employer to bargain in good faith with the union. The NLRB may also order employers to supply required information to the union during the collective bargaining process. When an employer terminates or alters its operation without negotiating with the union, the NLRB has ordered back pay, consistent with the same compensation provisions under sections 8(a)(3) and 8(a)(4), for the affected employees, when required.

If the NLRB finds flagrant or egregious violations in any of the above referenced areas, it can order extraordinary remedies. Such remedies include requiring the employer to mail the NLRB's orders directly to each employee's home or granting the union access to the employer's premises to post notices or meet with employees on nonwork time; none of which is normally required. The NLRB can also require the violating employer to pay litigation costs, attorney's fees and union expenses.

The NLRB's power is not omnipotent. There are some things it cannot direct an employer to do. For example, it cannot order an employer to make concession at the bargaining table, make violating the NLRA a crime, or adjudicate issues outside the six-month statute of limitations.

The best way for an employer to minimize exposure to adverse rulings by the NLRB is to conduct its employer/employee/union relations in such a fashion that violations will be minimized. This does not mean an employer must give up its right to manage its business. In fact, management has a duty to its stake holders to not abdicate its duty to the union or anyone else. Simply put, the employer duty to manage must be accomplished in a fair and ethical manner.

Mr. Hopkins is a member of SHRM's Employee and Labor Relations Committee.

CONSTRUCTION SITE SAFETY WHO IS RESPONSIBLE?

By: James H. Hopkins JD SPHR

I. Introduction

Employers in all industries must provide a safe work place. RCW 49.17.060.

The National Federation of Independent Business has compiled a list of the top 10 most common work place safety violations: (1) no written hazard communication plan; (2) no information and training on hazardous chemicals; (3) electrical conductors not protected entering boxes, cabinets, or fittings; (4) electrical covers on canopies missing; (5) tongue guards missing or not adjusted on abrasive wheel grinders; (6) hard hats not worn at construction sites; (7) lack of use of fall protection; (8) lack of fire extinguishers; (9) unsafe use of extension cords; and (10) failure to maintain safety records. This list contains items that may or may not be found at a construction site. These items result in the most citations for violation, but are simple to watch out for in any work environment.

II. Multiple Employer Work Site

When multiple Employers are involved, as on a construction job site, the site general contractor has a responsibility to insure compliance with the Washington Industrial Safety and Health Act (WISHA) for all Employees of all employers at the job site. Smith v. Myers, 90 Wn. App. 89 (1998).

It is the general contractor's responsibility to provide and/or require subcontractors to provide all necessary safety equipment for their portion of the work. Stute v. P.B.M.C., Inc., 114 Wn.2d 454 (1990).

Employees of a subcontractor can bring a negligence action against a general contractor without regard to the Workers' Compensation Statute. Stute v. P.B.M.C., Inc., Supra.

Not only can a general contractor have a negligence action brought against it by a subcontractor's employee, The Department of Labor and Industries (L&I), The State Department charged with enforcing WISHA, will issue safety citations to multiple contractors on a construction site.

L&I has defined the various Employers as:

1. The exposing Employer; the Employer whose Employees have been exposed to the hazard;

2. The creating Employer; the Employer who actually creates the hazard;

3. The controlling Employer; the Employer who has the authority (through contract or actual practice) to ensure the hazard is corrected; and

4. The correcting Employer; the Employer who has actual responsibility for correcting the hazard. WISHA Compliance Manual published by State of Washington, Department of Labor & Industries.

III. A General Contractors' Standard of Care

Neither the Courts nor L&I have established a standard of care for general contractors, which, when satisfied will keep the contractor from being issued a citation.

The Board of Industrial Insurance Appeals (BIIA) has accepted, the having of a safety program which is "effective in practice" as a defense to a citation.
Exxel Pacific Inc., 96 W182.

The BIIA has stated that a safety program is effective in practice when it discharges a contractor's "primary responsibility for job site safety."
Exxel Pacific Inc., Supra.

The first step in having an "effective safety program" is to have one in writing. The contractor must communicate all safety requirements and regulations to all at the job site and identify any safety hazards. Exxel Pacific Inc., Supra.

IV. Contract Indemnification Clause

Contractors routinely insert indemnification language in lower tier contractors' contracts, which require the lower tier contractors to indemnify the upper tier contractors from any damages caused by their failure to comply with WISHA or employee injuries. The following is an example of such a contract clause:
The Contractor shall indemnify and hold harmless the Owner, General Contractor, and agents and employees of them from and against claims for damages, losses and expenses, including but not limited to attorneys' fees, arising out of or resulting from performance of the Work, provided that such claim, damage, loss or expense is attributable to bodily injury, sickness, disease or death, or to injury to or

destruction of property, except those caused by the sole negligence of the General Contractor, its agents or employees, and/or caused by the negligent acts or omissions of the Subcontractor or anyone directly or indirectly employed by the Subcontractor.

Subcontractor specifically waives any immunity Subcontractor is entitled to pursuant to the industrial insurance statutes of the State of Washington, Title 51 RCW.

Such a clause is not enforceable as to the indemnitee's sole negligence. RCW 4.24.115(1). Such clauses are enforceable in concurrent negligence situations but only to the extent of the indemnitor's negligence, not the indemnitee's, and effective to waive any immunity under Washington Industrial Insurance Statutes. RCW 4.24.115(2). Gilbert H. Moen Co. v. Island, 128 Wn.2d 745 (1996).

V. Conclusion

Safety at the construction site is everyone's business and an important business. Not just from a monetary standpoint, but keeping individuals from being hurt is a worthwhile endeavor. Identifying the parties' responsibilities at the beginning of the project is the best method to protect against injury and L&I citations.

THE FAIR CREDIT REPORTING ACT (FCRA) AND THE INVESTIGATION OF EMPLOYEE MISCONDUCT

James H. Hopkins JD SPHR

There are many laws that govern the employer/employee relationship. These range from discrimination, safety, health and welfare to wrongful discharge. Employers must investigate allegations of harassment, hostile work environment charges of discrimination. An area an employer would not expect to look in the regulation scheme is the FCRA, unless of course the employer wanted a credit report. The FCRA regulates more than the age old credit report generated to determine if someone is paying their bills in a timely fashion. The FCRA governs investigative consumer reports, which go beyond the standard credit report and include any investigation done regarding a consumer i.e. employee, by an employer.

Investigative consumer reports are consumer reports covered by FRCA. These investigative consumer reports include reports regarding investigations of employee misconduct. What this means is when the employer use a third party to conduct the investigation the employee under investigation must be notified and permission obtain to obtain the investigative consumer report. Immediately several problems come to mind with the disclosure requirement. The question becomes can an employer conduct a confidential investigation into employee misconduct and/or conduct pre-employment investigations, the answer is yes, just that they must be made in compliance with FRCA. First and for most FRCA does not apply to investigation which are conducted by the employer itself. In addition FRCA does not apply when a third party, who is not in the business of providing such reports, does the investigation. This would be someone who does such investigation but it is not his or her principle business.

An employer may also provide a one-time disclosure and obtain permission from applicants and current employees for the employer to obtain a report at any time during the hiring process or during the employee's employment. When an employer takes this route it must make sure that the disclosure is clear and conspicuous.

ARTICLE NINE OF THE UNIFORM COMMERCIAL CODE MEETS CYBERSPACE

By: James H. Hopkins JD SPHR

Introduction

The revisions to article nine of the Uniform Commercial Code (UCC) expand definitions, allow for an expanded filing system and provide for additional perfection methods. This Article is based upon the 2000 amendments drafted by the committee of the American Law Institute and the National Conference of Commissioners on Uniform State Laws. Each State's Legislature may modify the model act when it adopts the revised Article nine or they may not adopt it at all, as of the summer of 2001, approximately 37 states had adopted the amendments. This Article will only cover certain modifications and the reader should review changes with an eye towards their specific circumstances.

Coverage of the modified Article nine

The modifications to article nine retain the current classifications of collateral, but; modifies them in some situations plus expanding and adding new classifications. Specifically software which is "embedded" in the hardware is a "good" along with the computer hardware. Computer hardware has always been defined as goods.

Software not "embedded" will be defined as an intangible.

Chattel paper, which is any writing that evidences both a monetary obligation and a security interest in specific goods, has been expanded. Chattel paper has been divided into, tangible chattel paper and electronic chattel paper. Tangible chattel paper is a writing on paper, while electronic chattel paper is a record stored on any electronic medium.

Attachment under the modified Article nine

Attachment of a security interest has basically remained the same under revised article nine as under previous amendments. Attachment of a security interest occurs when 1) value is given, 2) the debtor has rights in the collateral and 3)(a) the debtor has authenticated the security agreement or (b) the collateral is in the control of the creditor

Value: Value is defined the same as under a simple contract, the Court will look to whether there is consideration and not to whether there is sufficiency of consideration.

Control: The creditor has control of electronic chattel paper when the chattel paper is created, stored or assigned: 1) a single copy exists 2) the record identifies the secured party's interest 3) the secure party maintains possession of the record 4) any changes require the secured parties participation 5) any copies are identified as copies and 6) unauthorized copies are identifiable as such.

Authentication: A significant change with the modified article nine is the security agreement is to be "authenticated" not just have the signature of the debtor affixed as previously required. What the meaning of "authentication" specifically is not defined in the modifications, in fact the Official Comment which accompanies the modification states with all clarity "…represent the most basic of the evidentiary alternatives, under which the debtor must authenticate a security agreement that provides a description of the collateral". What this means to a Credit Professional is you must prove with whatever evidence you have that the debtor intended for a security interest to arise. As part of the security agreement the collateral must be described in such a manner as to be reasonably calculated as to identify the property. The security agreement must be filed in the State where the collateral is located.

A PRIMER ON PURCHASE MONEY SECURITY INTERESTS (PMSI) UNDER THE UNIFORM COMMERCIAL CODE
By: James H. Hopkins, Esq.

A purchase money security interest (PMSI) under the Uniform Commercial Code (UCC) is a security interest taken by 1) a supplier of collateral for the purchase price, or 2) a third-party lender who gives value so the debtor can purchase the collateral.

A PMSI can only be taken in goods and software -- it cannot exist in intangible products. In order for a PMSI to be created at all there must be a close nexus between the acquisition of the collateral and the secured obligation. A security interest will not qualify as a PMSI if you sell goods on an open, unsecured account, then subsequently attempt to create the security interest in the goods.

A PMSI:

1. Is automatically perfected in consumer goods.

2. In goods other than inventory, it is perfected when the creditor:

a. Has the debtor execute a security agreement authorizing the PMSI, and

b. Files a UCC-1 financing statement in the appropriate jurisdiction, within the time frame established by that jurisdiction, after the debtor takes possession of the goods.

3. In inventory, it is perfected when the creditor:

a. Has the debtor execute a security agreement authorizing the PMSI,

b. Files a UCC-1 financing statement in the appropriate jurisdiction before the debtor takes possession of the goods, and

c. Notifies existing secured creditors of record holding a security interest in the same type of inventory in which the creditor intends to take a PMSI. This must be done before the debtor takes possession of the goods.

Now, you may ask, "So what?"

Well, the "so what" is that a creditor with a properly perfected PMSI is entitled to a priority status ahead of previously perfected security interests covering after-acquired property. In addition when there are multiple PMSIs, a creditor holding a PMSI in the goods will have a priority over any third-party lender that may have a PMSI in the same goods.

What if the debtor has sold the goods and you hold a PMSI? Are you out of luck? Not necessarily. A PMSI in non-consumer goods extends to the identifiable proceeds from the sale of the goods against which the security interest is perfected. When the PMSI is in inventory, it extends to: 1) the identifiable cash proceeds received for the sale of the goods; 2) any chattel paper and/or instruments generated by the sale of the goods from inventory, if the secured party takes possession of the paper or instruments. Unfortunately, when the proceeds of the sale are deposited into a financial institution, the holder of the PMSI becomes subordinate to that institution's security interest. In addition, a PMSI in inventory does not extend to trade-ins or accounts receivable.

This article is based upon a general reading of the UCC, when, in fact, each state adopts the UCC for that state. With that in mind, you should verify the requirements for a PMSI in the states where you are selling goods, as there could be variations.

James H. Hopkins, Esq., was formerly General Counsel for Sicklesteel Cranes, Inc., and a member of Credit Today's Editorial Advisory Board.
Originally posted: May 2006. Reviewed and updated August 2016.

YOU TAKE THE GAVEL
BATTLE OF THE FORMS

By James H. Hopkins JD SPHR

The Facts of the Case:

The Buyer, a Delaware corporation with a New York residence, sends a purchase order to a Washington corporation, the Seller, whose residence is in Washington. The purchase order clearly identified the product, price and quantity. The purchase order was silent as to payment terms. In addition, it contained a clause calling for arbitration in the case of a dispute. The purchase order also stated Delaware law would apply and any disputes would be resolved in Delaware.

The Seller sent a confirmation of the order, within twenty-four hours of receiving the purchase order, which was silent as to whether arbitration was required and indicated Washington law applied and all disputes would be heard in Washington.

There was no response from the Buyer and the goods were shipped.

The Seller then sent an invoice, which stated "Net 30 Days" and had a 1-½ percent per month late fee.

Questions:

The questions are (1) Does an agreement even exist and, if so, what are the terms; (2) Is there an arbitration clause; (3); Are the payment terms net 30 with a 1 ½ percent per month late fee? (4) Does Washington or Delaware law apply and (5) are disputes to be heard in Delaware or Washington

Answers:

(1) Does an agreement even exist and, if so, what are the terms?

The Uniform Commercial Code (UCC), which applies to the sale of goods by a merchant, has altered the Common Law of contracts. Under the Common Law, there is the concept of the "mirror image rule", which means the acceptance of any offer must be a mirror image of the offer or it is a counter offer. The UCC will form a contract where it can be shown the parties wanted to form a contract and there was a "meeting of the minds" as to material terms of the contract.

A quick little check list to follow when determining whether a contract has been formed is: (1) did the Buyer express a definite and reasonable acceptance (r a confirmation sent within a reasonable time, which clearly accepts the offer even though it may contain additional or different terms); and, (2) did the Buyer's acceptance expressly assent to the Seller's offer without making agreement with the additional terms a condition of the contract formation. Following this checklist, I believe a contract was formed; leaving the only question as to what terms are included in the contract.

(2) Is there an arbitration clause?

Clearly, the arbitration clause will be part of the agreement as the acceptance was silent on this issue, meaning between the offer and the acceptance there was no dispute.

(3) Are the payment terms net 30 with a 1 ½ percent per month late fee?

The 30-days net and 1 ½ percent late fees will not be part of the agreement, as they were introduced after contract formation and were not part of the terms contemplated by the parties through the purchase order and acceptance.

(4) Does Washington or Delaware laws apply and where will disputes be heard in Delaware or Washington?

We now address the issue of which state's law applies and where will any dispute arising under this contract are held. Although there is no easy or clear-cut answer to this question, the analysis will be along these lines. When the clauses

between the offer and the acceptance conflict with each other, Courts will likely conclude that each party objected to the other party's conflicting terms and neither parties' terms will become a part of the contract. In our hypothetical situation, the application of law and venue clause language, will likely, not be part of the contract and New York, Delaware, Washington or some other state's law may apply depending upon the circumstances of the dispute.
Credit Practice Tip

The easiest procedure to follow to insure that language that one wants becomes a part of any give agreement, is simple review the documents and not just utilize preprinted forms that may or may not fit the situation.

YOU TAKE THE GAVEL
WHEN IS A PREFERENCE A PREFERENCE IN BANKRUPTCY PROCEEDINGS

By: James H Hopkins JD SPHR

The Facts of the Case:

The debtor made a payment for a bona fide debt to the creditor by check. The check was delivered to the creditor on November 18. The check itself was dated November 19, and the check was honored by the drawee bank on November 20. The debtor later filed bankruptcy. November 18 and 19 were the 92 and 91st day before the bankruptcy filing. November 20 was the 90th day before the bankruptcy was filed.

Under the Bankruptcy Code Subsection 547(b)1, 2, 3 and 4, any payment to a creditor for an antecedent debt made on or within 90 days of filing of a bankruptcy may be avoided by the bankruptcy trustee.

The question here is when was the payment made – on November 18, 19 or 20?

The Court's Ruling;

In Barnhill v. Johnson, the United States Supreme Court ruled that the transfer took place on the 20th, the date the drawee bank honored the check. The Court stated: ". . . receipt of a check gives the recipient no right in the funds held by the bank on the drawer's account. Myriad events can intervene between deliver of the check that would result in the check being dishonored. A third party could obtain a lien against the account by garnishment or other proceedings. The bank might mistakenly refuse to honor the check."

Credit Practice Tip

The Court clearly stated that when a check is delivered to the creditor, the time period to commence counting as to whether the payment as within the 90 day preference period does not begin to run until the check clears the debtor's bank. This raises a clear warning to credit managers that when working with a troubled debtor, payment should be made in a manner other than a check, or the check should be cleared with the debtors bank immediately.

YOU TAKE THE GAVEL

By: James H. Hopkins JD SPHR

The Facts of the Case:

While working on a federal construction project, a general contractor files for protection under the U.S. Bankruptcy Code. The general had provided a payment bond pursuant to federal statutes. In addition, the federal contracting body had withheld retainage from progress payments pursuant to the contract between the parties. As a subcontractor working directly under the general contractor, can you proceed with a foreclosure action against the bond and/or the retainage held by the contracting body?

The Court's Ruling

The retainage held by the contracting body is considered part of the general contractor's estate, and therefore the automatic stay would preclude the subcontractor from pursuing it without the bankruptcy court first granting relief from stay. In re Glover Const. Go Inc. 30BR873 (Bankr. Ky. 1985).

The general contractor is not a necessary party to an action on the bond by the subcontractor. The general contractor has neither a legal interest nor an equitable interest in the bond; it is for the benefit and use of the Federal Government. In re Jay Forni 33BR538 (Bankr. N.D. Cal. 1983). The bond would not be part of the general contractor's estate; therefore, an automatic stay would not preclude the subcontractor from commencing a foreclosure action pursuant to federal statutes. In re Capital York Construction Corp, V. Lynhaven Marine Construction Co. 43 BR 52 (Bankr. S.D.N.Y. 1984)

Credit Practice Tip

It is imperative that suppliers and subcontractors not only provide all notices required to perfect a claim, but also take steps to familiarize themselves with the individuals and companies with whom they do business. By implementing a sound credit policy, you may recognize a customer or general contractor who is in financial trouble before you commit to a large, and possibly an unrecoverable, account receivable.

YOU TAKE THE GAVEL

By: James H. Hopkins JD SPHR

The Facts of the Case:

You are the Credit Representative for a large wholesale distribution company. Your employer has a customer that has a significant receivable ninety days past due. The customer is a corporation, but the President of the corporation has personally guaranteed the debt.

The question is: does the Fair Debt Collection Practices Act ("FDCPA") apply to your collection efforts (1) as to the Corporation; (2) as to the President/personal guarantor? If not, why not?

Would your answer be different if you worked for a third-party collection agency? Why?

The Probable Outcome

The debt between the wholesale distribution company and the corporation clearly is a business debt, not a consumer debt. In this instance, the FDCPA would not be applicable, as it only governs consumer debt. The FDCPA does apply when a consumer is liable or allegedly liable for a debt. While it is true that the

President is a consumer who is liable or allegedly liable for a debt, the underlying debt is not covered. Therefore, the President's guarantee does not come within the purview of the FDCPA. Another limitation of the FDCPA is that it only applies to third-party collectors.

Although the FDCPA does not apply, a collector must still follow some principles of the Act in that they cannot use action that could be considered libelous, slanderous or an invasion of one's privacy when attempting to collect a debt. In addition, the Federal Communication Commission ("FCC") has taken the position that certain actions taken in the collection of a debt are prohibited when using the telephone. Calls made at odd hours, repeated calls or threatening calls to friends, neighbors or relatives, or calls that assert false positions are all prohibited. These activities are also prohibited under the FDCPA. In the event a collector violates these FCC directives, they may have their phone disconnected or face civil penalties.

Credit Practice Tip

A credit representative would be well advised to follow the guidelines outlined in the FDCPA in all collection matters. This will prevent individuals from having a cause of action against a collector regardless of whether the debt is for a consumer obligation.

YOU TAKE THE GAVEL TODAY WHEN "PAYMENT IN FULL" MEANS JUST THAT

By: James H. Hopkins JD SPHR

The law calls it "accord and satisfaction," but what exactly is it and when does it apply? Below are three different scenarios that will demonstrate how subtle, yet distinct, differences affect whether accord and satisfaction applies when a debtor pays a creditor.

A. Debtor owes creditor $10,000 on an open account. Debtor sends check for $8,000 with an endorsement on the back which states "Payment in full". Is this accord and satisfaction?

B. Debtor owes creditor $10,000; has called creditor on the phone and says, "I'm only going to pay you $8,000." Creditor does not acknowledge one way or another. Debtor sends the $8,000 with the restrictive endorsement "Payment in full". Is this accord and satisfaction?

C. Creditor and debtor are in a dispute as to returned goods.

Debtor owed creditor $10,000, but has indicated to creditor that $2,000 worth of goods have been returned and only $8,000 remains owing. Debtor sends a check for $8,000 with the restrictive endorsement "Payment in full". Is this accord and satisfaction?

HOW A COURT WOULD LIKELY RULE

An accord and satisfaction consists of: (1) a bona fide dispute between the parties; (2) an agreement to settle that dispute; and (3) performance on that agreement.

In order to have an accord and satisfaction, there must be an agreement separate from the agreement that established the debt in the first place. The parties must first have a meeting of the minds, basically all the elements of a new contract (i.e. offer, acceptance and consideration) before acceptance of a lesser sum than is owed will give rise to accord and satisfaction.

In our first scenario, there never was a meeting of the minds because there was no dispute; therefore, the creditor was never advised that the debtor believed $8,000 would satisfy the debt in full.

In the second scenario, accord and satisfaction could have been found had the creditor acknowledged there was a dispute over the amount owed, or taken any action which would have led the debtor to believe there was a dispute. If the dispute was clear to both parties and the creditor accepted the lesser amount with the restrictive endorsement, there is accord and satisfaction. As there was no acknowledgment by the creditor in this instance, there is no accord and satisfaction.

In the third scenario, there clearly is an accord and satisfaction. A bona fide dispute existed as to the dollar amount of the returned goods and the amount owed, and the debtor clearly put the creditor on notice that there was a dispute. By signing the limited endorsement, the creditor accepted the lesser amount as payment in full on the debt.

CREDIT PRACTICE TIP

As a practice, all checks should be reviewed front and back before being deposited. It is also recommended that when an account is opened for a customer, the first check received on that account be copied and kept in the debtor's file. All subsequent checks should be checked against that copy to monitor whether payment is being made by or from different accounts. Copies of checks from various accounts should be made and kept in the file.

A Credit Manager may want to implement this practice for two reasons: (1) when the debtor starts changing banks and bank accounts regularly, it indicate the debtor is having financial problems. However, the changes may be for other business reasons; therefore, a Credit Manager should not make a decision on this fact alone; and (2) in the event a judgment is obtained in a collection proceeding, the Credit Manager would seek to garnish those accounts of which he or she has knowledge first.

YOU TAKE THE GAVEL
WHEN IS A CONTRACT A CONTRACT

By: James H. Hopkins, JD SPHR

Case Scenario: A buyer contacts a seller of widgets and orders three dozen widgets at a price of $3.00 per dozen. The contact from the buyer is in the form of a Purchase Order (PO). The PO has terms and condition printed on the reverse side. The quantity and price is located on the front of the PO. The buyer's representative faxes only the front page of the PO to the seller, not the terms and conditions printed on the back. Based on the faxed copy of the PO, the seller shipped conforming goods. Before the goods are received the seller, but after the conforming goods were shipped, the seller faxed the buyer the terms and conditions printed on the reverse side of the PO. The terms and conditions placed requirements on the seller that the seller did not like, and the seller informed the buyer of the situation. The PO is silent as to when payment is due.

QUESTIONS:

1. Does the UCC apply?

2. Is there a contract?

3. Are the terms and conditions part printed on the back page of the PO part of the contract?

4. What are the payment terms of the contract?

ANSWERS:

1. Does the UCC apply? Yes.
In order for the UCC to apply, a "Transaction in Goods" needs to exist, which is the case in this transaction.

2. Is there a contract? Yes.
To be an enforceable contract, three basic elements must be present: (1) an offer; (2) an acceptance of the offer, and (3) consideration
.

Under the UCC an offer must be communicated to the offeree, (the seller in this instance) and its material terms must be specific (price and quantity are clearly spelled out in this case).

Acceptance of an offer by the offeree can be in any manner and by any medium reasonable under the circumstances. Shipping conforming goods would be a reasonable method of acceptance.

Consideration is the exchange of promises. Here, the buyer promised to pay and the seller promised to deliver conforming goods.

All three of the legs of an enforceable contract are present in this hypothetical situation-- offer, acceptance, and consideration.

    3. Are the terms and conditions printed on the back page of the PO part of the contract? Probably not.
    The short answer is probably not, for the contract was formed when the offer was accepted by shipment of the goods.

5. What are the payment terms of the contract? Past dealings or industry standards would dictate.
6.

To determine payment terms, the UCC looks to two areas to complete the contract's terms and conditions when, as in this hypothetical situation, the contract is silent. First, the UCC would require the parties analyze the past dealings between the parties. If there are none, then industry standards would be reviewed to determine the payment terms for this transaction.

YOU TAKE THE GAVEL

By: James H. Hopkins JD SPHR

Case Scenario: A creditor/seller ships non-consumer goods on open account to a debtor/buyer. After the goods leave the seller's possession, but before delivery to the buyer, the seller's Credit Manager, being a vigilant soul, discovers the buyer is insolvent.

Question(s): What are the Credit Manager's options under the following different scenarios:

(1) The buyer has not filed bankruptcy;

(2) The buyer has filed bankruptcy; and/or

(3) The buyer has filed bankruptcy and a financial institution has an Article 9 UCC filing, which includes those magical words, "all after acquired property".

Would the fact that the merchandise was consumer goods give the Credit Manager more options?

Answer(s):

(1) The buyer has not filed bankruptcy

The Credit Manager can look to Article 2-703 of the Uniform Commercial Code (UCC) at Section (1) which allows a seller to refuse delivery, except for cash, and stop delivery when the seller determines the buyer is insolvent. Section (2) of the same UCC Article allows a seller to reclaim delivered goods upon demand made within ten days of delivery when the seller discovers the buyer is insolvent. Whether the goods have been delivered will depend upon the contract between the parties.

If the contract calls for delivery to the buyer at the buyer's location (FOB buyer's warehouse), the goods could be stopped in route. In the event the goods have already arrived at the buyer's warehouse, the ten-day window to reclaim goods would begin to run from the date delivery was made.

If the contract calls for delivery to a common carrier (FOB common carrier), delivery to the buyer would be when the common carrier took possession of the goods. Under this scenario the demand to reclaim the goods must be provided to the buyer within ten-day of the seller providing the goods to the common carrier.

(2) The buyer has filed bankruptcy

The Credit Manager would still be able to stop goods in transit prior to delivery, however, the seller would more than likely be required to get approval of the Bankruptcy Court for the reclamation alternative of Section 2 of Article 2-207.

(3) The buyer has filed bankruptcy and a financial institution has an Article 9 UCC filing, which includes those magical words, "all after acquired property"

The situation changes when there has been a UCC filing granting a security interest to a lender in "after acquired goods". Goods that have been received by the buyer would qualify for this treatment.

The question then is: would the demand for reclamation authorized in Section 2 of Article 2-702 give a priority in those goods ahead of the party with the UCC filing with the "after acquired property" language? The answer is probably not.

The reclamation demand would be that of an unsecured creditor where the UCC filing grants a security interest in the "after acquired goods" which would have priority over the unsecured creditor.

For the seller to improve its position in such a situation, the seller could obtain a Purchase Money Security Interest defined at UCC Article 9-107. This would give the seller a security interest in the inventory sold by the seller (UCC Article 9-312), and would put the seller ahead of the secured party with the "after acquired property" language in its filing. The problem here is that the creditor must give notification to the holder of the blanket filing before the creditor files the PMSI or within 21 days after the goods are received by the debtor. Recording/filing the PMSI is not required if the goods are consumer goods.

In order for the PMSI to be a useful tool, the procedure of recording and notification must be done on all shipments. A creditor/seller must determine if this is practical for their particular business situation.

It cannot be said too often: There is no substitute for good credit evaluation.

www.ingramcontent.com/pod-product-compliance
Lightning Source LLC
Chambersburg PA
CBHW070316190526
45169CB00005B/1645